BYOB

CHICAGO

Your Guide to
Bring-Your-Own-Bottle
Restaurants and
Wine & Spirits Stores
in Chicago

3rd Edition

Jean Iversen

BYOB Chicago

Your Guide to Bring-Your-Own-Bottle Restaurants and Wine & Spirits Stores in Chicago, 3rd Edition

by Jean Iversen

Copyright © 2010 by BYOB Chicago, Inc.

BYOB Chicago[SM] is a servicemark of BYOB Chicago, Inc.

First Printing

Publisher, Author: Jean Iversen
Contributor: Michael Roper
Copyeditor/Proofreader: Sharon Sofinski
Interior, Cover, and Logo Design: Emily Brackett,
    Visible Logic, Inc. (visiblelogic.com)
Maps: Wendy Miranda
Photography (back cover): Paul Natkin (natkin.net)

Printed in the United States of America
ISBN 978-09764131-3-4
ISSN 1941-5443

BYOB Chicago, Inc.
P.O. Box 477803
Chicago, IL 60647
BYOB-Chicago.com

All of the information in the listings has been provided or con-firmed by the restaurants and wine & spirits stores in this book, and BYOB Chicago, Inc. assumes no responsibility for errors, inaccuracies, omissions, or any inconsistencies herein. In other words, if the stuff in this book isn't factual, it ain't our fault.

Contents

Publisher's Note

There's been a significant amount of change since I wrote the second edition of this book in 2006. "Top Chef," "The Next Food Network Star," and "Ramsay's Kitchen Nightmares" became huge hits on TV. Terms like *"Check, Please!* effect" and "foodies" are now part of our vernacular. Chefs are the rock stars du jour, starring in reality television series, publishing books, and judging cooking contests. There's no doubt about it: America is now a foodie nation. And Chicago is certainly a foodie town.

The spotlight on restaurants and the culinary arts has helped catapult the popularity of BYOBs to heights I never imagined. There are now nearly 400 BYOBs in Chicago-land—more than twice the number only five years ago. As the economy chokes and coughs, the news for BYOBs is better than ever. Restaurants are notorious for their high failure rate, yet Chicago's BYOBs are flourishing. Of the BYOBs in business in 2006, nearly 90 percent are still operating in 2009, and about 125 newcomers have joined the pack. It's safe to say that BYOBs are practically recession-proof. Plus, a restaurant that allows you to bring your own bottle no longer fits the stereotype of a Thai takeout joint in a strip mall. A BYOB policy is a selling point, reeling in foodies with discriminating palates and a well-stocked wine cellar. Nearly every episode of *Check, Please!* has one BYOB recommendation, and many restaurants in this book have been featured on the Food Network or in magazines such as *Food & Wine.*

The local wine industry also has seen an enormous amount of change in the last few years. The number of boutique wine stores in Chicagoland continues to increase. Several local wine shop owners have opened second, even third, locations—for example, Provenance, Pastoral, Lush Wine and Spirits, Galleria Liqueurs, and The Goddess & Grocer. New neighborhood wine shops have burst on the scene. Binny's has continued to grow, though retail giant Sam's Wine & Spirits changed hands and shuttered two of its stores. Online shopping has brought about huge shifts in consumer behavior, and most wine stores have followed suit with e-commerce options and shipping and delivery services.

It's unusual to write about business in a positive light right now. But BYOBs are more popular than ever *because* of our shaky economy. Like everyone else, Chicagoans are seeking ways to cut costs—but still yearn to dine out and forget the current state of economic affairs. In fact, history shows that businesses that offer entertainment value tend to flourish during a recession. What better way to lick our wounds without hurting our shrinking budgets than enjoying a great meal at a BYOB?

It's my pleasure to present the third edition of *BYOB Chicago*. Though a labor of love, this book was written during a time of more crises than I can count. Thanks to all who helped me through it. I especially want to thank my graphic designer, Emily Brackett, who helps make my decision to self-publish easy with her incredible attention to detail, reliability, and talent. Also, thanks to Sharon Sofinski, who contributed her copyediting and proofreading skills to an extremely tedious project; Michael Roper, who provided a refreshing article about the spirit of BYOB dining; and rock star Paul Natkin for my author pic. Thanks to all of you for making this the most painless edition to produce so far. I also want to thank my friends for their support and willingness to try new BYOBs. Thanks also to my family for their encouragement and faith. A special note goes to my father, whose entrepreneurial spirit I carry with me.

Cheers,

Jean Iversen
Publisher
info@byobchicago.com

About This Guide

Welcome to the third edition of *BYOB Chicago*. There have been numerous changes since the last edition, which was published in November 2006. About 50 BYOB restaurants have closed, but nearly 175 new ones have opened, and several new wine stores have been launched throughout the city and the suburbs. This edition contains listings for all of these new businesses and updated listings for existing ones. It also includes many new features that should prove useful when navigating Chicagoland's BYOB dining scene.

BYOB Chicago was first published in 2005. Over 20,000 copies of the book have sold since, and it has become the authority on Chicagoland's BYOB dining scene. The majority of restaurants in this book have consulted *BYOB Chicago* for guidance on corkage fees, etiquette, and other issues. The book is now available for use on your iPhone, Blackberry, and other mobile applications. It also is available for download to Kindle and other e-book technologies (see BYOB-Chicago.com for details).

There are now countless ways to access information about restaurants, from consumer-driven Web sites like Yelp.com, LTHForum.com, and Chowhound.com to local media. But it's important to note that, while some media are reputable sources of information, fewer are using primary sources for their content. More and more dining and entertainment writers gather their information from the Internet and other sources—in other words, they use secondary information, which is unreliable. In the publishing world, using primary resources is a golden rule. We never, for example, rely on Wikipedia to fact-check information. Wikipedia contains consumer-driven content that is not vetted by professional editors. There's only one way to gather information—whether it's for an entertainment feature or a hard news story—and that's going to the original source.

BYOB Chicago is a result of in-person interviews and visits to each BYOB restaurant and wine store. None of the information you have in your hands was gleaned from secondary sources or word-of-mouth. I met with nearly every business owner (a few were available only by phone) to accurately report their general information, menu, prices, future business plans, features, and BYOB policy. I believe this is the only way to write about food and wine. It was trying at times, especially in a city whose restaurateurs speak a variety of languages (and I don't), but ultimately it was a rewarding experience to meet the chefs and staff who run the diverse range of BYOBs in Chicagoland.

None of the BYOBs in this book have applied for a liquor license or have plans to do so. There are a few exceptions, but either their applications have been pending for quite some time or they vowed to not charge a corkage fee if and when a license is approved; these are noted. Otherwise, there are no "temporary BYOBs" in this book. All of the restaurants in this book not only allow but encourage their customers to BYOB.

Other than beverage service ratings, which are explained below, you'll notice that I don't offer a rating system for the food, service, or other qualities in "BYOB Restaurants A–Z" or "Wine & Spirits Stores A–Z." This may change in the future; for now, consider each listing a brief feature on each business.

As I mention in "375 BYOB Restaurants in Chicago-land—By Design or Default?" a BYOB policy is a selling point, especially in a rocky economy. These days, restaurants are doing everything they can to attract business; even hot dog stands and divey pizza joints are putting "BYOB" signs in their windows. I call these "incidental BYOBs," and they really are stretching the concept too far. I even saw one gas station takeout place touting "BYOB" in the window. I didn't include these, so you won't see any tiny taquerias, Internet cafés, convenience stores, or gas stations in the book.

What's New in the Third Edition

In the "BYOB Restaurants A–Z" section, I added some new features. First, a beverage-service rating applies to every restaurant (see "Key to Symbols Used" for a rating explanation). Knowing what type of accessories (wine glasses, corkscrews, ice, etc.) a BYOB offers makes it easier to plan accordingly. Other new features in this section? Each listing now indicates whether the BYOB charges a corkage fee or has a private party room (also listed in the index).

There are two new feature articles: one for trivia buffs, one for beer enthusiasts. In "375 BYOB Restaurants in Chicagoland—By Design or Default?" I reveal the reasons behind the growing BYOB phenomenon in Chicagoland. Discover why these restaurants are doing business without a liquor license; you may be surprised. And, never one to think only of wine when dining at a BYOB, I asked Michael Roper, owner of Hopleaf Bar, one of the city's most treasured brewpubs, to contribute a few words on BYOB dining. The result, "BYOB Dining: Experiment, Sample, Share," provides advice on selecting the finest brew(s) for your favorite BYOB, as well as insights on the best approach to BYOB dining.

And finally, I've raised the cap on corkage fees charged in "Restaurants That Allow BYOB for Corkage Fees of $0–$50." This section includes restaurants in all areas of the city and most suburbs, from casual joints like Leona's and Mama Thai to white-tablecloth eateries such as Blackbird and Avenues.

Newcomers

Each edition of *BYOB Chicago* features restaurants of a caliber more impressive than the last, evident in the growing number of chef-driven BYOBs. Find updated listings on such chef-driven BYOBs as Asian Avenue, Bonsoirée, Café Bella, Chilam Balam, Ciao Amore, Coast Sushi Bar, Côtes du Rhône, Couscous House, Dorado, HB Home Bistro, Hema's Kitchen, Los Nopales, Lucia's Ristorante, M. Henry, Marrakech Cuisine, May Street Café, New Tokyo, Pizza Rustica, Schwa, Semiramis, Shui Wah, Sticky Rice, Tanoshii, Terragusto, Toro Sushi, Treat, and Wholly Frijoles. Check out listings of the new chef-driven BYOBs in town: Café Marbella, Café 103, Café Orchid, The Grocery Bistro, Kapeekoo, Knew, Lan's, Mado, Mixteco Grill, Mythos, Radhuni, Real Tenochtitlan, Restaurant Sarajevo, Simply It, Smoque BBQ, Urban Belly, and Yassa.

The Italian thin-crust pizza trend continues, bringing new BYOBs like Antica Pizzeria, Ciao Amore, I Monelli Trattoria Pizzeria, Mista, Pizza by Alex, and Sapore di Napoli to the scene. Gourmet Mexican restaurants can't seem to keep up with demand. Standbys such as May Street Café, Dorado, and Wholly Frijoles continue to flourish, and newcomers Mixteco Grill, Real Tenochtitlan (license pending), and Chilam Balam are already serving capacity crowds.

Though Asian—especially Thai—BYOBs still dominate the book, there are a growing number of Mexican and BBQ places where you can bring your own bottle, as well as weekend brunch spots (see "BYOB Restaurants by Cuisine" index).

Closings

Since the last edition of the book, the following BYOBs have shut their doors: Afghan Restaurant, Ba Mien Viet Food Court, Buenos Aires Forever, Café Lao, Caliente (both locations), Calvin's BBQ, Caracas Grill, Chinoiserie, Cold Comfort Café, Crepes on Broadway, Curry House, Ecce Café, El Llano (Rogers Park), Fan Si Pan, Fierros, Jamaica Gates Restaurant, Japonica, J-Thai Sushi Bar and Thai Cuisine, Kabul House, La Cucina di Donatella, Nhu Hoa Café, North Coast Café, Orange (South Loop), Palmito's, Passage to India, Preaw Whan, Queen of Sheba Café, Ranalli's Up North, Rhythm and Spice, Rick's Café Casablanca, Rique's Regional Mexican Food, Rudy's Taste, Sai Mai Thai Restaurant, Sinbad's Fine Mediterranean Grill, Speakeasy Supper Club, Thai Me Up, Think, Tien Giang, Tom Yum Thai Cuisine, Tripi's Joint, Vien Dong, Wise Guys, and Wrightwood Skewers & Café. Many of these places have changed ownership but are still BYOB; the rest either have gotten a liquor license or remain vacant.

While all of the information was current as of press time, some of the details may change throughout the life of this book. If you know of a BYOB restaurant or wine store that isn't in the book but should be, please send an e-mail to info@byobchicago.com so that I can feature it in the future.

Enjoy this third edition—the largest to date—of *BYOB Chicago*!

—J.I.

375 BYOB Restaurants in Chicagoland—By Design or Default?

Alcohol is usually the largest profit center for any restaurant. There are 375 restaurants in this book. Three hundred and seventy-five eateries doing business without liquor licenses. But are these restaurants BYOB by choice? Or are they BYOB by default, hamstrung by obstacles that prevent them from selling food *and* drinks?

Before tackling this question, let's discuss some BYOB basics. In this country, the privilege of taking one's own alcohol to a restaurant is legal only in certain states, with Illinois being one of them. The laws governing BYOBs are complicated at best in other states, resulting in underground BYOBs in foodie-friendly cities like Boston and New York. And while toting your own wine is legal in California, the BYOB concept is not practiced throughout most of the state (except in wine country, where only industry insiders with rare vintages are allowed to bring bottles into well-stocked restaurants). Small pockets of BYOBs exist in Texas, which has several dry counties, and Washington, D.C., where the notion of bringing your own is gaining popularity.

However, Philadelphia is the only other U.S. city to boast a BYOB culture that rivals Chicago's. A liquor license will set back Philly restaurateurs anywhere from $20,000 to $250,000. The steep costs, coupled with Pennsylvania's complex state-controlled distribution system, have fostered a large number of BYOBs in the Philadelphia area.

With the fundamentals of BYOB laws covered, the original question remains: Are the restaurants in this book BYOB by choice? To find the answer, I asked each restaurant owner, "Why are you BYOB?" The answers fell into two main categories: by design and by default. Of 375 restaurant owners, 152 responded that their restaurant is BYOB by default, meaning that they would operate with a liquor license if certain restrictions were removed (a breakdown follows). But 176 indicated that they are, in fact, BYOB by design, or by choice. Some of these restaurateurs have even been approached by their alderman and encouraged to apply for a liquor license—approval guaranteed—but they turned it down. Surprised?

BYOBs by Design

Choosing to forgo a liquor license seems counterintuitive to running a profitable restaurant. But in the context of a troubled economy, when customers can choose between a good BYOB and a restaurant that charges a 200% to 500% markup on alcohol, the choice is obvious. Twenty-five owners whose restaurants are BYOB by design are using their BYOB policy as a selling point, especially during the recession. Another 20 claimed they are BYOB by design "for now" but may apply for a liquor license in the future "when things turn around." These eateries include Grocery Bistro, Machu Picchu, La Fonda del Gusto, and Estrella Negra, which are all waiting out the economic downturn and might tackle the city's complicated liquor license application in the future.

But the largest group of respondents in this category (44) claimed that they just want to focus on food, not a wine list. Newcomers like Antica Pizzeria, Côtes du Rhône, and Ciao Amore are willing to bet on a steady business of foodies bringing their own bottles. These places feel that they will not only survive but thrive as a BYOB—in any economy.

The other reasons restaurant owners cited for not wanting to sell alcohol include: religion (14); a health-conscious menu and/or philosophy (6); a breakfast or café concept (16); a family-oriented environment (24), a choice commonly voiced by the Asian community; and a focus on takeout and delivery, not dine-in, service (27).

BYOBs by Default

Many BYOBs in Chicago do not sell alcohol—by design. But that still leaves 152 others that are trying to turn a profit without a liquor license against their wishes (47 fell into both categories). Though these restaurants operate as BYOBs, it's not their first choice.

The number one reason for a default BYOB status? A municipal ordinance that prohibits any business from selling alcohol within 100 feet of a K–12 school, hospital, daycare center, home for the aged, library, or church. This ordinance accounts for 32 BYOBs in Chicago—restaurants like Tango Sur, Mythos, Jasmine Rice, and Ay Ay Picante. Coast Sushi was within 100 feet of a library when it opened, but that library moved. Plans to stock a full bar proceeded, until it was apparent that Coast's BYOB policy was one of its main selling points. Six years after opening, Coast Sushi proclaimed itself "BYOB for the long term."

Limited space (28) is another common reason for not being able to serve alcohol. These BYOBs simply lack the city's minimum space requirements for a bar, storage, refrigeration, taps, and glassware, and have no choice but to let their customers bring their own. "Too expensive," not surprisingly, was another top reason (26). The annual fee for a license ($2,200 in 2009, with a two-year minimum) isn't the only stopping point; the liability insurance and attorney's fees also stop small businesses in their tracks.

One Bathroom, No License

When it comes to serving alcohol, it's apparently necessary to have two bathrooms (one for men, one for women). Or so the city of Chicago says. Seventeen BYOBs claim only one bathroom and don't have any immediate plans to upgrade to the two required for a liquor license. So the next time you're at Treat, HB Home Bistro, or Terragusto and have to wait in line for the bathroom, just think: It could be worse. You could be paying a high markup on your drinks. Other BYOBs confided that their buildings weren't up to code (1), or that they had only one exit (1), which disqualifies restaurants from the liquor license lottery.

Woe to any restaurant in one of the city's dry precincts. Thanks to a local option referendum that permits voters in any Chicago precinct to vote their precinct "dry," they're all over the city. Since there are only about 14 BYOBs in dry precincts, it seems that most restaurants are avoiding these areas like the plague. Places like Café 103, Sikia, and Tre Kronor are all located in a dry precinct (so don't count on picking up a bottle near the restaurant).

Or, God forbid your lease prohibits you from selling alcohol. Five BYOBs cited this as the reason standing between them and a liquor license. Other reasons include: the restaurant is located in a Liquor Moratorium District (16); the owner is a Chicago police officer (1) or an alderman with a restaurant in his or her own ward (1), both of whom are prohibited from holding liquor licenses; the liquor license application was contested by at least 51% of all registered voters within 250 feet of the establishment (1); the license wouldn't transfer from the previous owner (6); or the owner or owner's spouse has a criminal record (3).

The rest of the restaurants in this book (47) are BYOB for a combination of reasons that fall under both the "by design" *and* "by default" headings. Most commented that going through the process of obtaining a liquor license is simply "too much of a hassle," that they are "worried about liability" or "uncontrolled underage drinking," that they are "worried about not turning tables," or have a perception, right or wrong, that a liquor license is too difficult to acquire and don't even bother trying.

Whether BYOB by design or by default, a recurring theme surfaced in these interviews with restaurant owners: In Chicago, especially in an uncertain economy, a BYOB policy is a selling point. Ten years ago, only a cult following chose to dine at the small number of BYOBs in Chicago. Today there are nearly 400 of these establishments—and a growing number in the suburbs—from chef-driven French bistros and upscale sushi bars to neighborhood Thai and BBQ joints. Not only are more and more Chicagoans seeking BYOBs, but restaurateurs are realizing that allowing customers to bring their own alcohol is a sustainable business model—in good times and bad.

—J.I.

BYOB Dining: Experiment, Sample, Share

by Michael Roper

BYOB restaurants allow us an affordable culinary adventure. Liberated from ordering drinks from a licensed restaurant whose owners typically think of the beverage program as the most important profit center, you can stretch your food dollars and enjoy cuisines you might not otherwise try. BYOBs also allow you to bring a more affordable adventure to the table in the form of a bottle—a beer bottle, that is.

First, you must plan ahead a bit. Many of the most interesting BYOB restaurants, particularly some of the ethnic ones, are located near packaged goods stores with the least interesting beer and wine selections. If you grab beer from these places, you may be stuck drinking Bud Light, hardly a beverage adventure. So make a stop at a quality beer shop. Since you are going to save quite a bit of cash on your meal at a BYOB, be willing to splurge a bit on the brew. Your favorite bar or licensed restaurant probably charges a markup of two and a half to three and a half times their cost. In a retail store, the margins are much slimmer. Use this opportunity to try that beer that costs $8.50 a bottle at the bar but only $2.99 or less retail. Some stores allow you to mix your own six-pack so you can try a variety of flavors. Going with a group? I strongly recommend 750 mL bottles that everybody can share. Many of the world's best beers come in this format.

Try to avoid the beer that is on the shelf next to the store window, exposed to the sun. Be wary of old beer on sale. Dusty bottles next to the heating vent? No, thanks. Brown bottles best protect the beer from the UV rays produced by fluorescent lighting. Beer stocked on lower shelves or behind other bottles is better protected from damaging light. Nothing is worse than sitting down to your meal at a BYOB with beer (or wine) that was poorly handled or is past its prime. The waiter can't take it back. You either have to live with it or go buy something else. Some beers age quite well, but in general it's best to drink them fresh. Check to see if there's a "best by" date on the bottle. When in doubt, ask the merchant how well the beer sells. If it's a good seller, it's probably fresh.

Why Drink Beer from a Glass?

Glassware is important. Never drink high-quality beer out of the bottle! The process of producing great-tasting beer is not finished until you pour it into a clean glass— right down the middle, creating a frothy head. As those bubbles pop, they release esters that you take into your nose. Remember, much of what beer offers us comes from our sense of smell. When you drink from the bottle, you cheat your nose and yourself out of half of the wonderful beer experience. You certainly would not drink that 2005 Bordeaux out of the bottle, and you should never drink a good beer that way, either.

If your BYOB choice has some sort of glass with a large surface area on top, use it. A wine glass also can be an excellent glass for beer. Sometimes when I bring a very special beer along to a BYOB, and I know the glassware options might not be ideal, I bring my own. It's one less glass for the dishwasher, so the restaurant staff usually don't mind. No matter what glass you use, though, it must be clean. Soap residue kills the frothy head and spoils the experience.

So, now for the question: what to bring? Many cuisines are far more beer- than wine-friendly. Beer is a natural pairing for spicy East Asian, Mexican, and Indian food. Beer is also very versatile. Fish, cassoulet, steak, oysters.... you name it, there's a great beer pairing available. I usually avoid the extremely bitter IPAs for subtly flavored foods. Belgian blonds, monastic brews and Saisons, continental-style pilsners, and American amber ales are all designed to pair well with food. Gueuze and wheat beers are great with salads, stouts or hoppy beers go well with cheese, pilsners with Indian. However, I believe that the main rule is that there are no rules unless you make them yourself. Try lots of flavor combinations. The more flavors that you bring to the table the better; a BYOB allows you to try more for a lot less. A pairing error is more palatable when it's a $2.50 bottle from a store instead of a $9 glass at a restaurant. Take chances. Try new things. Trust your own palate, not what you read in a book or in *Beer Advocate*. Above all, remember to have fun with your beer choices.

Finally, when I dine at BYOBs, I don't always bring beer or wine. Sometimes I bring both. For a multicourse meal, I may bring a dry, palate-cleansing, fizzy beer to start with and then alternate beer and wine depending on what the food calls for. I might bring cider, too. When I am in a shop, I might not know what I will order at the restaurant, so I come prepared. If I don't open everything I buy, it's no tragedy. That bottle will live to be drunk another day. I often bring my own bottle opener, so that I can open things when I am ready. More choices, more fun, and for far less money. BYOBs offer a terrific chance to broaden our food and beverage horizons and, in particular, to bring good beer to the dining table—where it belongs.

Michael Roper is the owner of the Hopleaf Bar in Chicago, one of the city's finest brewpubs. Roper has taught beer-related courses at The Siebel Institute, Kendall College, Le Cordon Bleu Culinary School, and Loyola University. In 2005 he was inducted into Le Chevalerie du Forquet des Brasseurs in Brussels (The Knighthood of the Brewers Mash Staff), which is the ancient Brewers' Guild of Belgium. For more information on Hopleaf and its latest expansion, go to hopleaf.com.

BYOB
Restaurants

Key to Symbols Used

PRICES
$ = average entrée costs $10 or less
$$ = average entrée costs $11–$15
$$$ = average entrée costs $16–$20
$$$$ = average entrée costs over $20

BEVERAGE SERVICE
no stars = no corkscrews, bottle openers, ice, or glassware available

★ = corkscrews, bottle openers, water glasses or plastic/foam cups available

★★ = corkscrews, bottle openers, ice, wine glasses available

★★★ = corkscrews, bottle openers, ice buckets, wine glasses, and one or two types of specialty glassware available*

★★★★ = corkscrews, bottle openers, ice buckets or chillers, white and red wine glasses, and several types of specialty glassware available*

*Specialty glassware includes Champagne flutes, pilsner glasses, beer mugs, margarita glasses, shooters, rocks glasses, martini glasses, sake cups, sake pitchers, snifters, and others.

SYMBOLS
🚭 No corkage fee
🔫 Corkage fee
🏖 Outdoor patio
🍷 Private party room
🅿 Parking available
💵 Cash only
🏧 ATM on premises

BYOB
Restaurants A–Z

ADESSO $$$ / ★★★
3332 N. Broadway (Buckingham), Lakeview
Italian/Brunch

Dave Jones (Tutto Pronto/Adesso in the Gold Coast) offers rustic Italian in casual, chic surroundings on a hip strip of shops, cafés, bars, and restaurants. Choose from antipasti, salads, soups, pastas, and *carni e pesci*. No corkage fee for beer or spirits.
(773) 868-1516, Mon–Fri 11–10, Sat 10:30–11, Sun 10:30–10

ALOHA EATS $ / -
2534 N. Clark (Deming), Lincoln Park
Hawaiian

This place has been hailed as one of President Obama's favorite eateries in Chicago. Their specialty is mixed plates—plates piled high with scoops of rice, macaroni salad, and meat (the Hawaiian version of comfort food). And yes, that's Spam on the menu; apparently it's a Hawaiian staple. There's also katsu, pulled pork, BBQ short ribs, and grilled or fried fish.
(773) 935-6828, alohaeats.com, Mon–Thurs 11–10, Fri–Sat 11–10:30, Sun 11–9 ⊛

ALWAYS THAI $ / ★★
1825 W. Irving Park (Ravenswood), North Center
Thai

Former Arun chef Rungravee Kusub sold this reliable neighborhood Thai spot, so the celeb cache is gone, but new owners haven't made any noticeable changes to the menu, cute decor, or anything else. And with a liquor store conveniently located a couple of doors down, they're not planning on getting a liquor license anytime soon, either.
(773) 929-0100, Mon–Fri 11–10, Sat 4–10, Sun 5–9 ⊛

AMELIA'S $$$ / ★★★
4559 S. Halsted (46th), Back of the Yards
Mexican/Brunch
Chef Eusevio Garcia (Mundial-Cocina Mestiza) and cousin
Leo Garcia are behind this BYOB, which features Central and
Southeastern Mexican–influenced cuisine (mussels in chipotle
white wine butter sauce, ceviche, sautéed shrimp in green mole).
Virgin sangria and margarita mixes are available. (Their liquor
license may be in the works, so call ahead to make sure they're
still BYOB.)
(773) 538-8200, Mon–Thurs 11–10, Fri–Sat 11–11, Sun 10–9 ☂

AMIRA'S TRIO $ / ★★
3047 N. Cicero (Barry), Northwest Side
Cuban/Puerto Rican
Chef/owner Vicky Amira recreates the traditional Puerto Rican
and Cuban recipes she grew up with at this casual neighborhood eatery. Try dishes such as *ropa vieja* (shredded marinated
beef) from the Cuban side and *jibarito* (grilled steak and onions
sandwiched between fried plantains, not bread) on the Puerto
Rican. Nonalcoholic sangria mix is available.
(773) 205-6200, amirastriorestaurant.com, Sun–Tues 11–8, Wed
closed, Thurs 11–8, Fri–Sat 11–10 ♿ ☂

ANDALOUS MOROCCAN $$$ / ★★
3307 N. Clark (School), Lakeview
Moroccan
This ethnic neighborhood place is the only BYOB in Lakeview to
offer Moroccan cuisine. Choose from a variety of kebabs, tagines
(slow-cooked stews), couscous entrées, and *pastille*, a Moroccan
mix of garlic, cheese, spices, and vegetables or meat in phyllo
dough. No more hookahs (due to smoking ban).
(773) 281-6885, andalous.com, Mon–Thurs 4–10, Fri 4–12, Sat
11–11, Sun 11–10, reservations recommended ♿ ☂

ANN SATHER $ / ★★★
909 W. Belmont (Clark), Lakeview
Scandinavian/Brunch
The last few years represent a lot of change for this Scandinavian
breakfast landmark: Alderman Tom Tunney now owns all four
locations; the Belmont location no longer serves dinner; and after
decades at its original location, it moved a few doors east to this
new space (American Apparel now inhabits the old address).
The original artist was flown in from Norway to recreate the
hand-painted wall murals, and staff transplanted the original
chandeliers, recreating the charm of the previous site with an
updated feel. While the menu offers several American items,
Ann Sather's still serves its famous cinnamon rolls and Swedish
pancakes with lingonberries (to do otherwise would create an
uprising). For brunch goers, there's nonalcoholic Bloody Mary
mix, fresh strawberry/banana/orange juice, and other fresh juices
to blend with your own vodka or Champagne.
(773) 348-2378, annsather.com, Mon–Fri 7–3, Sat–Sun 7–4
⊛ ⍨ Ⓟ

ANN SATHER CAFÉ $ / ★★★
3411 N. Broadway (Roscoe), Lakeview
Scandinavian/Brunch
(773) 305-0024, Mon–Fri 7–3, Sat–Sun 7–4 ⊛

ANN SATHER $ / ★★★
3416 N. Southport (Roscoe), Lakeview
Scandinavian/Brunch
(773) 404-4475, 7–2 daily ⊛ ⛱

ANN SATHER $ / ★★★
5207 N. Clark (Foster), Andersonville
Scandinavian/Brunch
(773) 271-6677, Mon–Fri 7–2, Sat–Sun 7–4 ⊛

ANONG THAI $ / ★★
2532 N. California (Altgeld), Logan Square
Thai

The new owner opened Anong (named after his mother, and
which translates to "beautiful lady" in Thai) on Obama's inau-
guration day as a tribute to the 44th prez. With all menu items
under $10, this place could be considered part of Logan Square's
stimulus package. So stock up on the *lumpia* petite rolls, crab
Rangoon, papaya salad, curries, and panang noodles.
(773) 292-5007, anongthai.com, Mon–Thurs 11–9:30, Fri–Sat
11–10:30, Sun 11–9 ⊛

ANTICA PIZZERIA $$$ / ★★
5663 N. Clark (Hollywood), Edgewater
Italian

Antica's 800-degree wood-burning oven produces light, crispy, yet
chewy pizzas (choose from *margherita*, *quattro formaggi*, *salame*,
and others). A classic selection of antipasti, salads, pastas, and
entrées rounds out the menu. Decanters available on request.
(773) 944-1492, Mon–Thurs 5–10:30, Fri–Sat 5–11:30, Sun
5–9:30, reservations recommended on weekends ⤙

AROY THAI $ / ★
4656 N. Damen (Leland), Ravenswood
Thai

Aroy's 67-item menu carries the usual array of Thai apps, soups,
salads, noodle and rice dishes, curries, and entrées found
elsewhere in Chicago. However, the expanded choices of meat
with each dish (tofu, chicken, pork, beef, boneless duck, crispy
catfish, shrimp, or squid) easily separate Aroy Thai from the pack.
A daily special menu is handwritten in Thai and posted next to
the kitchen.
(773) 275-8360, 11–10 daily ⊛

ASIAN AVENUE $–$$$ / ★★★
1624 W. Belmont (Ashland), Lakeview
Japanese/Thai

Sushi chef/owner Alan Julamoke spent several years honing his craft at Sushi Wabi before opening this exceptional Asian spot, where he also features his mother's Thai recipes. Fish is delivered here every other day for the *hotategai* (seared scallops with apple and plum puree), maki moni (the midori dragon and volcano are dramatic in presentation), and sushi entrées. Julamoke also runs Late Night Thai, just a few doors down, to satisfy the after-hours crowd.
(773) 549-2201, latenightthai.com, Mon closed, Tues–Sat 11:30–10, Sun 11:30–9 ☻

ASIAN MIX CAFÉ $ / ★
3945 N. Broadway (Irving Park), Lakeview
Pan-Asian

This tiny neighborhood takeout place serves an impressive mix of Thai, Chinese, and other Asian-influenced favorites. Though service is focused on carryout and delivery, there is a 16-seat dine-in area in which to BYOB. Choose from curries, lemongrass pork, Mongolian beef, pad Thai, fried rice, and several soups, salads, and appetizers.
(773) 857-0989, asianmixcafe.com, Mon–Fri 11:30–10, Sat 12–10, Sun 4–10 ☻

ATLAS CAFÉ $$ / ★★
3028 W. Armitage (Whipple), Logan Square
Eclectic

Students hang out at this café during the day, tapping away at laptops and sipping bottomless cups of joe. But at night, musicians and appreciators come to hear the open mic on the first Tuesday of the month and live jazz on Wednesdays. The kitchen serves up a wide range of snacks and entrées, from bruschetta to Grecian salad to empanadas and kebabs.
(773) 227-0022, 11–10 daily ☜

AY AY PICANTE $$$ / ★★
4569 N. Elston (Kennicott), Mayfair
Peruvian
Ceviche, jumbo shrimp, and seafood entrées dominate the menu
at this lively Peruvian spot. Their location, which is across the
street from a church, prohibits Ay Ay Picante from getting a liquor
license. But if a recent remodeling job and a new, lush, 32-seat
garden patio in the back are any indication, it looks like their
BYOB status is working for them.
(773) 427-4239, ayaypicante.com, Sun–Thurs 11–10:30, Fri–Sat
11–11 🐝 🏴

AZHA $ / ★★★
960 W. Belmont (Sheffield), Lakeview
Thai
With all of the sleek sushi/Thai combo spots popping up around
town, there's something refreshing about a good ole neighborhood
Thai joint. Azha's menu is filled with classic Thai recipes (save for
the "Drunk Man's Special," a noodle dish that wins the best-
named dish award). A skylight perks up the otherwise ho-hum
interior, and they have surprisingly good beverage service (chilled
beer mugs, pilsner and wine glasses).
(773) 525-0555, Mon–Thurs 11–10, Fri–Sat 11–11, Sun 4–9 🐝

B AND Q AFRO ROOT CUISINE $$ / ★
4701 N. Kenmore (Leland), Uptown
African
You may have seen B and Q's food trucks around the city. But if
you haven't been to their restaurant lately, you're in for a pleasant
surprise. They've moved to a new location and updated the decor
with hardwood floors, soft drapes, white linen tablecloths, and
leather chairs, transforming this business from drab carryout to
destination BYOB.
(773) 878-7489, bqafrorootcuisine.com, Mon–Sat 11–10, Sun
12–10 🐝

BABYLON EATERY $ / ★★
2023 N. Damen (McLean), Bucktown
Middle Eastern
Owners' plans to obtain a liquor license fell through, and the
state's smoking ban took away their hookah service. But neither
setback has deterred this casual Bucktown place from maintaining its popularity with the neighborhood. Most likely it's due to
the excellent, made-to-order food, seasoned and marinated to
perfection. This is quite possibly one of the best Middle Eastern
spots in town.
(773) 342-7482, Mon–Sat 11–10, Sun 11–9 🖐 🎏

THE BAGEL $$ / ★
3107 N. Broadway (Briar), Lakeview
Jewish/Brunch
Chicagoans know The Bagel (open since 1950) for its authentic
Jewish breakfast and deli. But this place also serves more than a
dozen dinner entrées, available à la carte or as four-course meals.
Choose from broiled whitefish, liver and onions, brisket, and
sides like kishke, potato pancakes, and noodle pudding.
(773) 477-0300, bagelrestaurant.com, Mon–Thurs 8–10, Fri–Sat
8–11, Sun 8–9 🖐 Ⓟ

BALKAN RESTAURANT $ / ★★
2321 W. Lawrence (Claremont), Lincoln Square
Eastern European
New management took over this Old World–style eatery in 2008,
but expect the same menu, which features cuisine from the
former Yugoslavia. If you're not sure what to order, try the *sarma*
(meat mixed with rice and cabbage), *chevapi* (beef sausages), or
bureek (meat with cheese and spinach in a pastry dough). Crepes
are served all day; order off the menu or build your own.
(773) 878-7764, Mon–Sat 7–8, Sun 7–5 🖐 Ⓟ

BAMBOO GARDEN $ / ★
3203 N. Clark (Belmont), Lakeview
Chinese

With the proliferation of Thai and sushi spots around Chicago, there are fewer and fewer traditional Chinese restaurants around, especially the dine-in variety. But six days a week (they're closed on Mondays), this clean, sparse place, with peach-colored walls, terra-cotta floors, and Chinese wall hangings, serves a wide variety of mostly Mandarin Chinese (egg foo yong, moo-shu pork), including a wide selection of vegetarian options.

(773) 281-9000, Mon closed, Tues–Sun 11–11 ⊛

BARBERRY PAN ASIAN KITCHEN $ / ★★
2819 N. Southport (Diversey), Lakeview
Thai

New owners took over in 2008 but kept the focus on high-volume delivery and takeout service (thus no liquor license). There are only a few seats downstairs, but upstairs there's seating for an additional 14 (perfect for small private parties). As of press time, street parking was pay box– and permit-free, so enjoy the freebie while you can.

(773) 525-6695, 11–10 daily ⊛

BEN TRE CAFÉ & RESTAURANT $$ / ★★
3146 W. Touhy (Kedzie), West Rogers Park
Vietnamese

Located in a small shopping plaza in a dry precinct, Ben Tre is a casual Vietnamese eatery that offers an alternative to busier Argyle Street. With over 100 choices on the menu, you might want to browse your options online before you go.

(773) 465-3011, Sun–Tues 11–9:30, Wed closed, Thurs 11–9:30, Fri–Sat 11–10 ⊛ Ⓟ

BEN'S NOODLES AND RICE $ / ★★
1139 W. Bryn Mawr (Winthrop), Edgewater
Thai
This charming diner offers classic Thai dishes to keep tradition-alists happy (chicken satay, tom kha, pad Thai) and a few choices for the slightly more adventurous (basil roasted duck, stir-fry beef with mushrooms in oyster sauce, fried banana). There's also fried rice and teriyaki for diners who are less enamored with Thai food.
(773) 907-8936, bensnoodlesandrice.com, Mon–Tues 11–9, Wed closed, Thurs 11–9, Fri–Sat 11–10, Sun 12–9 ⊛

BHABI'S KITCHEN $$ / ★★★★
6352 N. Oakley (Devon), West Rogers Park
Indian/Pakistani
This celebrated BYOB has tripled in space since it opened nearly 10 years ago, no doubt due to the demand for Bhabi Syed's homestyle butter chicken, freshly baked breads (20 in all), and vegetable samosas (this author's favorite). Just about every type of glassware is available. The owners were looking for a new location at press time, so call ahead to confirm their address.
(773) 764-7007, Mon 1–10, Tues 5–10, Wed–Fri 1–10, Sat–Sun 12–10, reservations recommended ⊛

BIG PHO $ / ★
3737D W. Lawrence (Ridgeway), Albany Park
Vietnamese
Located in a no-frills shopping plaza, this is a spacious, modern spot for slurping huge bowls of *pho* (beef broth packed with herbs and various combinations of beef, seafood, chicken, and vegetables). For a real meat lover's special, go for the "big *pho*," a blend of meatballs, flank steak, brisket, and tripe.
(773) 478-8282, Mon–Sat 10–9, Sun closed ⊛ Ⓟ

BIRCHWOOD KITCHEN $ / ★
2211 W. North (Leavitt), Wicker Park
Eclectic/Brunch

Daniel Sirko and Judd Murphy (Pastoral) teamed up for this
gourmet sandwich spot in the former Cold Comfort space, which
they've completely remodeled. Barred from a liquor license
because of the church next door, they serve sandwiches and
salads made with seasonal ingredients and artisanal breads from
the ubiquitous Red Hen Bakery.
(773) 276-2100, birchwoodkitchen.com, Mon closed, Tues–Fri
10:30–9, Sat–Sun 9–4 ⊗ 🠖

BITE CAFÉ $ / ★★
1039 N. Western (Augusta), Ukrainian Village
Eclectic/Brunch

With only one bathroom, Bite is ineligible for a liquor license. No
problem; just walk through the adjoining door to music venue
Empty Bottle, belly up to the fully stocked bar, and walk back
to your table with a microbrew, a glass or bottle of wine, or your
favorite cocktail. (See emptybottle.com/about.htm for hours and
"booze" list.) Or, bring your own. The seasonal menu rotates
every few months. There are also daily specials and a popular
weekend brunch.
(773) 395-2483, emptybottle.com/bite.htm, bigbitesite.com,
Sun–Thurs 8–10:30, Fri–Sat 8–11:30 ⊗

BLUE ELEPHANT $ / ★★
1235 W. Devon (Magnolia), Edgewater
Pan-Asian

This cute, casual spot, run by the same family as Shiso (a BYOB in
Lincoln Park), is a solid neighborhood place for lunch and dinner.
The "Blue Specials" include dishes such as salmon green curry
pasta and the wok-tossed blazing shrimp and scallops. No hard
alcohol allowed, only beer and wine.
(773) 262-5216, elephantkitchen.com, Sun–Fri 11–10,
Sat 4–9 ⊗ 🠖

BONSOIRÉE $$$$ / ★★★
2728 W. Armitage (California), Logan Square
Eclectic

Chef Shin Thompson's popular underground Saturday night
dinners attracted such a following that a full-time restaurant
was in order. Now fans can enjoy Thompson's inventive cuisine
several nights a week in a Japanese-inspired, 26-seat dining room
(a beautiful outdoor patio accommodates 26 more). Bonsoirée
offers four-course, seven-course, and 13-course menus, which run
$45, $85, and $150, respectively. The menu rotates seasonally
and takes advantage of locally sourced produce, and meats and
seafood from all over the world. Saturdays are still invite-only
(join their e-mail list to be notified) and feature a six-course tasting menu that revolves monthly. Check the Web site for a current
menu and suggested wine pairings. Decanters and wine chillers
are available on request.

(773) 486-7511, bon-soiree.com, Mon closed, Tues–Fri 5–10, Sat
invite only, Sun seasonal, reservations recommended ⊛ ⋗

BORINQUEN $$ / ★
1720 N. California (Wabansia), Humboldt Park
Puerto Rican

Juan "Peter" Figueroa has owned and operated this family-oriented joint for nearly 20 years, and it if weren't for the school across
the street, he'd be serving drinks alongside *papas rellenas* (stuffed
potato balls) and *lechon* (roasted pork). Borinquen may expand
to another location and secure a liquor license in the near future.
Until then, Puerto Rican families and neighborhood regulars will
continue to pack this no-frills place, which boasts selling over
100 of their famous *jibaritos* (a sandwich served on fried green
plantains) daily.

(773) 227-6038, borinquenjibaro.com, Sat–Thurs 10–10, Fri
10–11 ⊛

BRASA ROJA $$ / ★
3125 W. Montrose (Troy), Albany Park
Colombian

You can't miss this place—just look for the rows of juicy rotisserie chickens spinning around in the front window. Whole and
half chickens come with potatoes, plantains, corn pancakes, or
cassava. There's also red snapper, catfish, beef brisket, steaks,
chops, and ribs. Owners (El Llano) remodeled and expanded to
the space next door, so if you haven't been here in a while, it's
worth a visit.

(773) 866-2252, labrasaroja.com, 9–10 daily ⊛

BUENA VISTA RESTAURANT $ / ★
3147 N. Broadway (Briar), Lakeview
Mexican

This charming, 24-seat spot is a solid choice for homemade,
made-to-order Mexican food, whether it's *chilaquiles* for breakfast,
sopes pastor for lunch, or carne asada and shrimp fajitas for
dinner. Nothing fancy or trendy here, just authentic flavors, fresh
ingredients, and reasonable prices, all of which have been keeping
regulars coming back for over 15 years.

(773) 871-5782, buenavistarestaurantinchicago.com, Mon–Sat
11–11, Sun 11–10 ⊛ ⚑

BUTTERFLY SUSHI BAR & THAI CUISINE $$ / ★★
1156 W. Grand (May), River West
Japanese/Thai

Butterfly has filled a niche in Chicago: high-quality sushi, moder-
ate prices, and a contemporary yet unpretentious atmosphere.
Customers pack it in nightly for the fresh fish (ordered daily) and
inexpensive, solid Japanese and Thai dishes from the kitchen. The
modern decor and subdued clubby background music appeal to
a mostly younger crowd, though Butterfly draws neighborhood
regulars as well.

(312) 563-5555, butterflysushibar.com, Mon–Thurs 11–10, Fri
11–11, Sat 12–11, Sun 12–10, reservations recommended ⊛ ⚑

BUTTERFLY SUSHI BAR & THAI CUISINE $$ / ★★
1421 W. Chicago (Noble), West Town
Japanese/Thai
This West Town offspring has a smaller space but offers the
same menu and ambience as the original. For a truly decadent,
delicious, and inexpensive meal, try the sesame chicken. For less
than $10, you'll get a deep-fried chicken breast stuffed with fried
egg, spinach, sesame seeds, and crabmeat, with peanut sauce and
rice on the side. I dare you to finish it.
(312) 492-9955, butterflysushibar.com, Mon–Thurs 11–10, Fri
11–11, Sat 12–11, Sun 12–10, reservations recommended ⊛ ⤢

BUZZ CAFÉ $$ / ★★
905 S. Lombard (Harrison), Oak Park
American/Brunch
Every Friday is "Burgers, Bands, and Beers," when you can
bring your own brews, listen to live music, and dine on organic
gourmet burgers. BYOB is also welcome at weekend brunch and
on weeknights. Buzz offers daily dinner specials and a wide menu
of mostly organic flatbreads, sandwiches, and entrées.
(708) 524-2899, thebuzzcafe.com, Mon–Fri 6–9, Sat 7–9, Sun
8–2 ⊛ ⤢

CAFÉ BELLA $$ / ★★★
3311 W. Fullerton (Spaulding), Logan Square
Eclectic/Brunch
By day, this neighborhood café serves coffee drinks, sandwiches,
and wraps. But at night the place transforms, offering a gourmet
dinner menu created by ex-Ambria sous chef Cesar Casas. Three
different entrées are featured every weekend, from duck to lamb
shank to swordfish, most with a Latin or Caribbean influence.
Nothing is ever fried.
(773) 292-5040, cafebellaonline.com, Mon–Sat 11–10,
Sun 9–10 ⊛

CAFÉ BLOSSOM $$$ / ★★
608 W. Barry (Broadway), Lakeview
Japanese

Just off of busy Broadway, Café Blossom is a relaxing alternative
to other Lakeview eateries—especially their charming sidewalk
patio. Highlights from the menu include the maki rolls, like the
baked volcano (salmon, whitefish, crab), the salsa (spicy tuna,
cilantro, avocado, jalapeno, tempura crumbs), or specials, which
rotate weekly. The intimate dining room seats 15, and five more at
the sushi bar. No sake bombs allowed.

(773) 935-5284, cafeblossom.com, Mon–Sat 4:30–11, Sun closed
⊛ ⚑

CAFÉ CENTRAL $$ / ★
1437 W. Chicago (Bishop), West Town
Puerto Rican

Though the surrounding neighborhood has radically transformed
in recent years, Café Central (thankfully) hasn't changed much
since it opened in 1950. Buffet-style Puerto Rican dishes still
tempt diners from behind the old-fashioned counter (complete
with barstools). The dining area has ample seating for dining on
plantain sandwiches or one of the dozens of seafood-based soups
and entrées.

(312) 243-6776, 9–9 daily ⊛

CAFÉ CON LECHE $$ / ★
1732 N. Milwaukee (Wabansia), Wicker Park
Mexican/Brunch

This newcomer serves up flavorful Mexican fare (think *pechuga
poblana*, not greasy burritos) in an updated, cheerful space. The
tiny kitchen turns out surprisingly ambitious entrées such as
roasted pork with rice and charbroiled marinated skirt steak.
Brunch is served Saturdays and Sundays from 7–3.

(773) 342-2233, cafeconlechebucktown.com, 7–10 daily ⊛ ⚑

CAFÉ COREA $$ / ★
1603 E. 55th (Cornell), Hyde Park
Korean

In an area brimming with Thai eateries, this authentic Korean joint is a breath of fresh air. Café Corea serves an authentic, not watered-down, version of fiery dishes such as kimchi and *bulgogi*. BYOB is not terribly common (bring your own stemware if a water glass is inadequate), but it is welcome.

(773) 288-1795, Mon–Fri 11:30–9, Sat 12–9, Sun closed ⊛

CAFÉ FURAIBO $$ / ★★★
2907 N. Lincoln (Diversey), Lakeview
Japanese

Furaibo ("wanderer" in Japanese) opened as a takeout/delivery spot (thus no liquor license). But the demand for dine-in service grew, so now it's a popular BYOB. Their specialty is maki rolls (44, to be exact), with fire drops, furaibo, Caribbean secret, and red typhoon among the most popular. There are also appetizer and entrée portions of hibachi-broiled shrimp, scallops, steak, and chicken. No corkage fee with entrée.

(773) 472-7017, cafefuraibo.com, Mon–Thurs 11:30–10, Fri 11:30–11 (closed Mon–Fri 2:30–5), Sat 5–11, Sun 4–9

CAFÉ HOANG $ / ★
1010 W. Argyle (Sheridan), Uptown
Thai/Vietnamese

You will find the following suggestion, courtesy of Café Hoang's chef and owner, either offensive or helpful: Vietnamese usually like menu item #20 (spicy beef noodle soup), and "the Americans" usually like items #22–#27 (combo meals with an egg roll, noodles, mixed veggies, and choice of grilled meat). Not convinced? Proceed at your own risk.

(773) 878-9943, cafehoang.com, Mon–Sat 10–10:30, Sun 10–10 ⊛

CAFÉ HOANG $ / ★★
232 W. Cermak (Wentworth), Chinatown
Thai/Vietnamese
Owned by the same family that runs the Argyle Street location, this Chinatown offshoot offers the same Thai/Vietnamese combo menu that's heavy on the latter. Families, tourists, and regulars keep the kitchen busy with a regular stream of hot pots, lemongrass, *pho*, and *bún* (vermicelli noodle). Unlike other Chinatown BYOBs, Café Hoang has a few wine glasses and corkscrews available on request.
(312) 674-9610, Mon 10:30–10, Tues closed, Wed–Thurs 11–10, Fri–Sun 12–10:30 ⊛

CAFÉ MARBELLA $$$ / ★★★
3446 W. Peterson (Bernard), Northwest Side
Spanish
Virgilio Trujillo (Arco de Cuchilleros) and Enrique Segni are behind this Sauganash culinary gem, which features authentic Basque- and Catalonian-influenced tapas and entrées. If their kitchen keeps cranking out dishes like the bacon-wrapped figs with brandy cream sauce and Rioja potatoes and sausage, this place won't be a well-kept secret for long.
(773) 588-9922, cafemarbella.com, Mon closed, Tues–Thurs 11–9:30, Fri 11–10, Sat 5–10:30, Sun 4–9 ⊀

CAFÉ MEDITERRA $ / ★★
728 S. Dearborn (Polk), South Loop
Eclectic
This charming neighborhood café—complete with locally produced artwork for sale—serves a tasty breakfast and lunch menu to area businesses by day, a casual dinner to neighborhood regulars at night. Locals enjoy Mediterranean-influenced "specialty plates" (kebabs), sandwiches (falafel, wraps), flatbreads, and entrée-sized salads.
(312) 427-2610, cafemediterra.com, 7–9 daily ⊀

CAFÉ 103 $$$$ / ★★★
1909 W. 103rd (Wood), South Side
Contemporary American/Brunch
Anyone who says Beverly lacks a fine-dining BYOB hasn't tried
Café 103. Open since 2007, owners Blair and Shirley Makinney
offer a rotating menu based on local, seasonal ingredients. The
Makinneys sell virgin Bloody Mary, mojito, margarita, and martini
mixes next door at their grocery, Beverly's Pantry. They encourage
you to bring them to Café 103 to blend with your own vodka,
gin, or tequila.
(773) 238-5115, cafe103.com, Mon–Tues closed, Wed–Sat 11–3,
5–10, Sun 9–2 ✦

CAFÉ ORCHID $$ / ★★
1742 W. Addison (Lincoln), Lakeview
Turkish
Co-owner and chef Kurt Serpin did stints at A La Turka and Café
Istanbul before opening this neighborhood treasure. Half of the
vast menu is devoted to appetizers such as eggplant musakka and
skewered mussels. Then it's on to entrées such as shish kebabs
and *uskudar*, tender lamb cubes sautéed with garlic and veggies
and wrapped in eggplant.
(773) 327-3808, cafeorchid.com, Mon–Thurs 11–10, Fri–Sat
11–11, Sun 5–10 ⊛ Ⓟ

CAFÉ SOCIETY $ / ★★
1801 S. Indiana (18th), South Loop
Eclectic
Located in the Prairie District, this casual coffee-and-dessert café
has a stunning outdoor courtyard and two dining areas inside.
Owners would prefer that you choose one of their coffee drinks or
smoothies, but BYOB is welcome. The lunch/dinner menu is a mix
of sandwiches, wraps, burgers, burritos, salads, and appetizers.
(312) 842-4210, Sun–Wed 7–5, Thurs–Sat 7–11 ⊛ ☂

CAFÉ SUSHI $$ / ★★★
1342 N. Wells (Evergreen), Old Town
Japanese
This Old Town spot is known for its classic Japanese menu
(gyoza, katsu, teriyaki) and "sushi boats," an assortment of
sashimi, rolls, and sushi presented on large, wooden ships. To
keep up with evolving tastes, however, the menu features more
and more maki and specialty rolls. No corkage fee with a $15
minimum food purchase per person in parties of six or more.
(312) 337-0700, Mon–Thurs 1–10, Fri–Sat 1–11, Sun 1–9 🐾

CAFÉ TOO $$$ / ★★
4715 N. Sheridan (Leland), Uptown
Contemporary American/Brunch
Students at this café's culinary skills job training program cook
and serve lunch and dinner under staff supervision. A prix fixe
menu is available for dinner; dishes rotate weekly and range from
summer squash fritters to roast beet salad and ancho-glazed pork
loin. Check the Web site for current hours.
(773) 275-0626, cafetoo.org 🐾 🐾

CAFÉ TRINIDAD $$ / ★★
557 E. 75th (Rhodes), South Side
Caribbean
The menu at this Chatham BYOB features cuisine from Trinidad
and Tobago, which is influenced by Jamaican, Caribbean, African,
and Creole cooking. Daily specials include dishes such as okra
and rice with spinach, pumpkin and chicken, Trinidad curry crab
dumplings, and *callaloo* (creamy spinach and okra). Live entertainment on the weekends.
(773) 846-8081, cafetrinidad.com, Mon–Thurs 11–8, Fri–Sat
11–9, Sun 12:30–7 🐾

CAFFE FLORIAN $ / ★★
1450 E. 57th (Blackstone), Hyde Park
American/Italian/Brunch
This is the type of neighborhood place that locals dine at several
times a week. With an eclectic menu (crab cakes, chicken
marsala, pork chops, pastas, and their famous sausage, pesto, and
spinach pizza), there's something for everyone. Ingredients are
always fresh, the vibe comfortable.
(773) 752-4100, florian57.com, Mon–Thurs 11–9:30, Fri–Sat
11–10, Sun 10–9:30 ⚞

CARO MIO ITALIAN RISTORANTE $$$ / ★★★
1827 W. Wilson (Wolcott), Ravenswood
Italian
Fresh flowers and flickering candlelight set the stage for an
intimate, romantic setting at this neighborhood BYOB, which carries an extensive Italian menu that will leave your mouth watering
before the bread comes. Find familiar Italian staples—gnocchi,
risotto, veal, calamari—homemade pastas, and several vegetarian
options. Reservations taken for six or more.
(773) 275-5000, caromiochicago.com, Mon–Thurs 4–10, Fri–Sat
4–11, Sun 3–9, reservations recommended ⊛ ♥

CASBAH CAFÉ $$$ / ★
3151 N. Broadway (Briar), Lakeview
Middle Eastern
Norair Yacoubian is the second-generation owner of this neighborhood gem (the original location opened in 1962 at 514 W.
Diversey). Many of the same recipes still appear on the menu, like
the kafta kebab, falafel, and kibbeh. Sea scallops, steak Madagas-
car (beef tenderloin sautéed in cream-brandy sauce), couscous
entrées, and many Middle Eastern apps round out the rest of the
menu. Regulars keep their own stemware in-house; bistro-style
wine glasses also available.
(773) 935-3339, Sun–Thurs 5–11, Fri–Sat 5–12 ⚞

CEDAR'S MEDITERRANEAN KITCHEN $$ / ★★
1206 E. 53rd (Woodlawn), Hyde Park
Middle Eastern

Located in the Kimbark Plaza, Cedar's offers a sleek, beautifully designed dining room, gallery-style kitchen (smoke-free, due to the state-of-the-art hood), and a wide-ranging Middle Eastern menu. Choose from flatbreads made in their stone oven, combo platters, kebabs, *shawerma*, and couscous.
(773) 324-6227, eatcedars.com, Sun–Thurs 11:30–10, Fri–Sat 11:30–11, reservations recommended on weekends ⊛ Ⓟ

CEMITAS PUEBLA $ / ★
3619 W. North (Monticello), Humboldt Park
Mexican

Featured on Food Network's *Diners, Drive-ins and Dives*, this is as much a gathering place as a restaurant: Regulars hang out, watch *futbol*, and crack open a couple of cold ones. They also chow on the house specialty, *cemitas*, a sandwich that originated in Puebla, Mexico, and is made with sesame seed bread, avocado, adobo chipotle peppers, Oaxacan cheese, and meat.
(773) 772-8435, cemitaspuebla.com, 11–9 daily ⊛

CHAI THAI BISTRO $$ / ★★
4748 W. Peterson (Cicero), Northwest Side
Thai

This cute, contemporary Sauganash spot boasts a larger-than-expected menu, from the same owners as Evanston's Noodle Garden. There are a few surprises, like the Thai roasted chicken with papaya and sticky rice, deep-fried lime chicken, maki rolls, and beautifully presented banana wonton dessert.
(773) 481-0008, chaithaibistro.com, Mon–Thurs 11:30–9:30, Fri–Sat 11:30–10, Sun closed ⌇

CHARLEY THAI PLACE $ / ★★
3209 W. Armitage (Kedzie), Logan Square
Thai
If you like Thai Linda Café (a Thai BYOB in Roscoe Village),
you'll find something strangely familiar about Charley Thai. That's
because husband-wife team Charley and Linda feature the same
menus at their respectively named eateries. The dishes are not
quite as Americanized as those in other Thai joints, evident in
dishes like the spring rolls and sweet basil.
(773) 278-3200, lindacharleythai.com, Sun–Mon closed, Tues–
Thurs 11–9:30, Fri–Sat 11–10 ✧

CHILAM BALAM $$$ / ★★
3023 N. Broadway (Barry), Lakeview
Mexican
Local phenom Chuy Valencia, a 23-year-old graduate of Le
Cordon Bleu's California Culinary Academy, is behind this new
BYOB. Valencia, raised with the Californian farm-to-plate mental-
ity that's now taking hold in the Midwest, worked his way up at
Frontera Grill, Topolobampo, and Adobo before opening this cozy
spot. Expect a seasonal menu with updated versions of Mexican
classics, like grilled pork ribs with Oaxacan pasilla glaze, halibut
ceviche, and grilled game hen with charred tomato *molcajete* salsa.
(773) 296-6901, chilambalamchicago.com, Sun–Mon 5–10, Tues
closed, Wed–Thurs 5–10, Fri–Sat 5–11 ⊛

CHINESE KITCHEN $ / ★★
1007 W. Argyle (Sheridan), Uptown
Chinese
It seems that half of all the restaurants on this strip of Argyle have
changed hands in the last few years. Chinese Kitchen—a small,
casual spot—is just one of many newcomers, offering a full menu
of Szechuan, Hunan, and Mongolian cuisine. A cozy dining area
is available if you wish to dine-in and BYOB.
(773) 271-4140, Mon–Sat 11–12, Sun 4–12 ✧

CHOPAL KABAB & STEAK $ / -
2240–42 W. Devon (Bell), West Rogers Park
Indian/Pakistani

The ornate wood-carved furniture, artwork, and screens were imported from Pakistan to give this comfortable place an authentic feel. Customers are mostly Muslim families gathering together to share heaping plates of beef kebabs, chilli chicken (chef/owner Khawaja Ali's special recipe), naan, and seafood. BYOB is "low profile," so only one bottle allowed per table.
(773) 981-3338, 12–12 daily ⊛ Ⓟ

CHUTNEY JOE'S $ / ★
511 S. State (Congress Pkwy.), South Loop
Indian

After a 25-year sabbatical from the restaurant biz, Vijay Puniani developed this "fast-casual" concept that relies on slow-cooked, homestyle Indian food. No premade sauces or saturated fats are used (samosas are baked, not deep-fried, and no cream in the chicken tikka masala). Expect more locations soon.
(312) 341-9755, chutneyjoes.com, Mon–Thurs 11–9, Fri–Sun 12–9 ⊛ ⊁

CIAO AMORE $$$ / ★★★★
1134 W. 18th (May), Pilsen
Italian

This beautiful, 100-seat *ristorante* is the brainchild of Gus Drugas and Cesar Pineda (Caro Mio) and offers upscale cuisine at comfortable neighborhood prices. Expect traditional dishes such as calamari, bruschetta, and handmade pastas as well as beef shank, mahi-mahi, and homemade lobster ravioli in arribiata sauce with jalapenos. Proper dress required.
(312) 432-9090, Mon closed, Tues–Thurs 11–10, Fri 11–11, Sat 4–11, Sun 3–9 ⊛

CJ'S EATERY $$ / ★
3839 W. Grand (Avers), Humboldt Park
American/Brunch
The menu at Charles Armstead and Vanessa Perez's sunny spot
is based on American comfort food but ventures into Cajun and
Latin territories with excellent results. With only one bathroom,
they're stuck with the BYOB policy (for now), but their devoted
following doesn't seem to mind.
(773) 292-0990, cjs-eatery.com, Mon–Wed closed, Thurs–Fri 8–9,
Sat–Sun 9–9

COAST SUSHI BAR $$$ / ★★★
2045 N. Damen (Armitage), Bucktown
Japanese
This elegant, "nouvelle Japanese" BYOB serves fresh, inventive
sushi, maki (the white dragon signature maki alone is reason
to come here), and appetizers and entrées to a capacity crowd
almost every night. To placate complaining neighbors, only one
bottle of wine or sake or one six-pack of beer is allowed per
couple, and no hard alcohol is permitted.
(773) 235-5775, coastsushibar.com, Mon–Sat 4–12, Sun 4–10,
reservations recommended ✆

CÔTES DU RHÔNE $$$$ / ★★
5424 N. Broadway (Balmoral), Edgewater
French
When chef/owner Brian Moulton moved here from Massachu-
setts, he looked for a casual neighborhood French bistro in his
Edgewater neighborhood, but none existed—so he opened up his
own. Taking over a former Mexican restaurant, Moulton painted
the interior warm chocolate brown, added mood lighting, and
created a pared-down French bistro menu. A BYOB serving escar-
got? Yes. Cassoulet? Of course. And pate, a cheese plate, seafood
Provençale, French onion soup, and roasted rack of lamb. With
all dishes made-to-order and all pan-sauced, this is destination
dining with a casual, come-as-you-are vibe. Crème brulee and
other tempting desserts may entice you to bring a dessert wine.
(773) 293-2683, Mon–Tues closed, Wed–Thurs 6–10, Fri–Sat
6–11, Sun 6–9:30 ✆

COUSCOUS $ / ★★
1445 W. Taylor (Laflin), University Village/Little Italy
Middle Eastern/Moroccan
Due to a state ordinance that prohibits liquor licenses within 100
feet of schools, nearly every restaurant on this block of Taylor
Street is BYOB. The menu features both Middle Eastern (falafel,
kebabs, kibbeh) and Maghreb cuisine, or couscous dishes made
with chicken, fish, or lamb. Be sure to save room for the homemade baklava.
(312) 226-2408, couscousrestaurant.com, Mon–Thurs 11:30–9,
Fri 11:30–11, Sat 12–8, Sun closed ⊛

COUSCOUS HOUSE $$ / ★
4624 W. Lawrence (Knox), Northwest Side
Mediterranean
Chef Sammy Abbas recreates his Algerian mother's recipes, all
made with imported Moroccan couscous, at this casual spot.
Couscous entrées, Middle Eastern dishes, and dinner salads
compose most of the menu, but the daily tagines (slow-cooked
North African, Algerian, Egyptian, and Moroccan stews) are the
highlight. Mama would be proud.
(773) 777-9801, Sat–Thurs 11–10:30, Fri 3–10:30 ⊛

COUSIN'S INCREDIBLE VITALITY $$ / ★★
3038 W. Irving Park (Sacramento), Albany Park
Vegetarian
Owner/chef Mehmet Ak ran Cousin's, a Mediterranean restaurant
in Lakeview, for years, then switched to an all-raw diet to counter
health problems. Today, Cousin's is a raw food emporium,
catering to health-conscious individuals with a Mediterranean-
influenced restaurant, retail store, classes, and prepared foods to
go. Ak doesn't drink, but allows his customers to BYOB.
(773) 478-6868, cousinsiv.com, 11–10 daily ⊛

COZY NOODLES & RICE $ / ★
3456 N. Sheffield (Cornelia), Lakeview
Thai
Owner Tee Meunprasittiveg displays his vast assortment of collectibles, filling this tiny spot with hundreds of Pez dispensers, vintage toys, and old radios; the tables are even converted vintage sewing machines. The food is fresh, tasty, quick, and cheap (don't skip the baby egg rolls).
(773) 327-0100, cozychicago.com, Sun–Thurs 11–10, Fri–Sat 11–10:30 ⊛ ⚑ Ⓟ

COZY NOODLES & RICE $ / ★
1018 Davis (Maple), Evanston
Thai
Collections of vintage lunch boxes and toys, hurricane lamps, and license plates provide plenty of eye candy at this second location, where a doting staff serves contemporary Thai fare at recession-friendly prices. Go early; Northwestern students, neighborhood regulars, and first dates fill up this place at dinnertime. Servers will give you corkscrews and glasses but won't touch your bottles if they are underage. No hard alcohol.
(847) 733-0101, cozyevanston.com, Mon–Thurs 11:30–9:30, Fri–Sat 11:30–10, Sun 4–9:30 ⊛

CRISP $ / ★
2940 N. Broadway (Wellington), Lakeview
Korean
New owners took over Rice Box, updated the decor with fresh, bright colors, and created a fun, contemporary menu of updated Korean fare, served cafeteria-style at large communal tables. Regulars rave about the Korean fried chicken—especially the jumbo wings with BBQ or hot sauces of varying degrees of heat (all the way to buffalo suicide). There are also modern versions of *bulgogi* and kimchee.
(773) 693-8653, crisponline.com, Mon closed, Tues–Thurs 11:30–9, Fri–Sat 11:30–10:30, Sun 11:30–9 ⊛

D'CANDELA $$ / ★★
4053 N. Kedzie (Belle Plaine), Albany Park
Peruvian
There aren't many Peruvian eateries in Chicago, so this newish
neighborhood spot is a nice surprise. In a casual, diner-like
atmosphere, owner Luis Perez serves up rotisserie chicken and
seafood-based Peruvian appetizers, soups, and entrées. Start with
empanadas or ceviche, then move on to breaded steak, Peruvian-
style chicken, or fried tilapia.
(773) 478-0819, Mon closed, Tues–Thurs 11:30–9, Fri–Sat 11:30–
9:30, Sun 11:30–9 ⊛

DE PASADA $ / ★
1517 W. Taylor (Laflin), University Village/Little Italy
Mexican
This no-frills diner serves up traditional Mexican breakfast, lunch,
and dinner to a diverse, ever-changing neighborhood (though the
budget-friendly menu appeals especially to the student population). Choose from standard offerings such as tacos, burritos,
tortas, and gorditas, as well as a half dozen or so dinner plates
(carne asada, chile rellenos, breaded steak).
(312) 243-6441, Sun–Thurs 7–11, Fri–Sat 7–12 ⊛

DHARMA GARDEN $ / ★★
3109 W. Irving Park (Albany), Irving Park
Thai/Vegetarian
Since 2003, this place has served healthy Thai (no MSG, no
meat, only filtered water used in cooking) in a large space filled
with Thai artifacts. However, they've recently added a few
chicken dishes in addition to the usual imitation duck and tofu
offerings, and the dining room has been partitioned in half to
accommodate a private party room. For something off the beaten
path, try one of their seafood or vegetarian dishes, like the sweet
corn vegetable cake.
(773) 588-9140, Mon 4–11, Tues–Sat 11–11, Sun 12–11 ⊛ ☙

DIB $$ / ★★★
1025 W. Lawrence (Kenmore), Uptown
Japanese/Thai

This location has had a new owner in each edition of this book, but Dib is positioned for staying power. The interior has been completely revamped with a contemporary, clean look, and a seasoned chef is stationed at the sushi bar. There are plenty of wine glasses, sake cups, and Champagne flutes on hand to help wash down the creamy crab maki or Japanese entrées.

(773) 561-0200, Mon–Thurs 11:30–10, Fri–Sat 11:30–10:30, Sun 12–10 🥢 Ⓟ

DORADO $$$$ / ★★
2301 W. Foster (Oakley), Ravenswood
Nuevo Latino

Trying to pigeonhole the cuisine here would be a mistake. With a background in both Mexican and French cooking, chef/owner Luis Perez fuses the two and achieves outstanding results. While the duck nachos remain the house favorite, don't forget about the inventive entrées (crunchy almond crusted trout, grilled pork chop with plum mole sauce) or the crab cakes with guacamole and smoked chipotle tomato sauce.

(773) 561-3780, Mon closed, Tues–Thurs 5–10, Fri–Sat 5–11, Sun 5–9, reservations recommended on weekends 🍴 Ⓟ

DOUBLE LI $$ / ★
228 W. Cermak (Wentworth), Chinatown
Chinese

Ben Li is the gracious chef/owner of this 40-seat spot near the Red Line's Cermak/Chinatown stop. Li honed his chops at culinary school in Szechuan, where he also owned his first restaurant. Now Li brings his hot and spicy cuisine to Chinatown. Highly recommended: the dumplings appetizer (steamed pork dumplings in chili oil, scallions, and soy sauce) and the black pepper garlic beef tenderloin.

(312) 842-7818, Sun–Thurs 10:30–9:30, Fri–Sat 10:30–10:30 🥢

DRAGON COURT $ / ★★
2414 S. Wentworth (24th), Chinatown
Chinese

Live lobsters and crabs beckon from their tanks at the front
window of this established neighborhood eatery. There are also
live scallops and clams, daily soups, seasonal specials, and the
famous house spiced crispy half chicken. Most of the menu appeals to American tastes, but a "secret" Chinese menu is available
on request. A wide assortment of stemware is available, left by the
previous owners, who had a full bar.

(312) 791-1882, 11–2a daily ☯

DUCK WALK $ / ★
919 W. Belmont (Sheffield), Lakeview
Thai

"The tiny place with the cool wall mural" is the best way to
remember this cozy Thai spot, wedged in between other Lakeview
BYOBs, record stores, and clothing boutiques. The food is fresh
and tasty, and service is friendly and very quick. This isn't a place
to hang and drink that second bottle of Pinot Noir, though; space
is tight and table turnover is the name of the game. But plenty of
bars are nearby to continue the party.

(773) 665-0455, duckwalkchicago.com, Sun–Thurs 11–10, Fri–Sat
11–11 ☯

ECUADOR RESTAURANT $$ / ★★
2923 W. Diversey (Richmond), Logan Square
Ecuadorian

Until recently, Ecuadorian restaurants were practically nonexistent
in Chicago. Now, our city boasts several, including this cute,
family-owned, brightly painted spot. Dinner options include daily
specials for less than 10 bucks and entrée-sized soups brimming
with seafood or skirt steak (served with beans, rice, potatoes,
and plantains). If you can wash all of that down with a few beers,
more power to you.

(773) 342-7870, Wed–Mon 11–9, Tues closed ☯

ED'S POTSTICKER HOUSE $ / ★★
3139 S. Halsted (31st), Bridgeport
Chinese
Owners Brenda and Ed Yu make an annual trek to China to scout
out fresh new recipes, then incorporate them into the menu at
this Bridgeport gem. All of the noodles are handmade on-site, and
spices and bean pastes are imported from China, so expect fresh,
well-seasoned, authentic cuisine. Choose from dim sum or over
100 menu options (or something from the "secret menu," which
caters to traditional Mandarin tastes). Plans for a liquor license
may be in the works, so call ahead.
(312) 326-6898, Mon–Thurs 11–10, Fri 11–11 ⊛

EDWARDO'S $ / ★
1321 E. 57th (Kenwood), Hyde Park
Italian
Edwardo's trademark dish is stuffed pizza with cheese and
spinach. Over the years they've added an "international line of
pizzas," like the Tex Mex, Hawaiian Luau, and Spicy Buffalo.
There are also pastas, calzones, sandwiches, and salads. Most of
Edwardo's locales serve alcohol, but this one's BYOB since it's in a
dry precinct.
(773) 241-7960, edwardos.com, Sun–Thurs 11–10, Fri–Sat
11–11 ⊛

EL LLANO RESTAURANT $$ / ★★
3941 N. Lincoln (Irving Park), Lakeview
Colombian
Even in the middle of a weekday afternoon, this cute place is
packed with families, cops, and tradesmen. Owned by the same
folks as Brasa Roja (famous for its rotisserie chicken, which is
not offered here), El Llano serves up generous plates of South
American–style steaks, pork chops, and chicken, all served with
sides of potatoes, fried plantains, rice, cassava, or salad. Daily
specials such as steak or chicken with rice, beans, and salad ring
up for only $4.95.
(773) 868-1708, Sun–Thurs 11–10, Fri–Sat 11–11:30 ⊛

EL PRESIDENTE $$ / ★
2558 N. Ashland (Wrightwood), Lincoln Park
Mexican

A father-daughter team is behind this 24-hour eatery, which serves homestyle Mexican food. Everything is made from scratch daily, including the *pico de gallo* and rice and beans. Prices are low, portions are enormous (the gorditas appetizer is enough for a meal), and with a school across the street, they're BYOB indefinitely. Only beer or wine allowed; no hard alcohol.
(773) 525-7938, elpresidenterestaurante.com ⊛ ⤳

EL RINCONCITO CUBANO $ / -
3238 W. Fullerton (Sawyer), Logan Square
Cuban

The food takes center stage at this no-frills, hectic neighborhood diner. Regulars feast on *ropa vieja* (shredded beef in tomato sauce), *masas de puerco* (fried pork), and daily specials elbow-to-elbow at the counter or at checkered-tablecloth four-tops. The atmosphere is a heady mix of animated Spanish, ringing registers, and *tostones* frying in oil.
(773) 489-4440, 11–8:30 daily ⊛

EL VENENO MARISCOS $$$ / ★
1024 N. Ashland (Cortez), East Ukrainian Village
Mexican

El Veneno Mariscos features the cuisine of Nayarit, Mexico, which means myriad seafood dishes (crab legs, shrimp wrapped in bacon, red snapper, oysters, marlin). In case that's not apparent, the fishing nets, life rings, and wooden ships that adorn the walls will remind you.
(773) 252-7200, Mon–Thurs 10–10, Fri–Sun 10–11 ⊛ ⤳

EL VENENO MARISCOS $$$ / ★
6651 S. Pulaski (67th), South Side
Mexican

One of three locations (the third is in Georgia), the mantra at this cozy, nautical-themed West Lawn spot is "yesterday in the ocean, today in your hands." There's a limit of three *cervezas* per person at both Chicago locations.
(773) 582-5576, Mon–Thurs 10–10, Fri–Sun 10–11 ⊛ ℗

THE ELEPHANT $ / ★★
5348 W. Devon (Minnehaha), Northwest Side
Thai
The food at this Edgebrook BYOB is made-to-order with fresh ingredients, genuine Thai spices, and no MSG. One of the house favorites is the grilled Thai sausage, made with ginger, roasted peanuts, and chilies. Daily specials are listed on a chalkboard at the entrance.
(773) 467-1168, http://elephantthaicuisine.com, Mon–Sat 11–9, Sun closed ⊛

EN•THAI•CE $ / ★★
5701 N. Clark (Hollywood), Edgewater
Thai/Vegetarian
Owner/chef May Tareelap has won over the neighborhood with this casual spot. You'll find classic Thai favorites on the menu, and May is happy to customize most dishes for vegans. They provide full beverage service (unless the server is underage).
(773) 275-3555, Mon closed, Tues–Thurs 11–9, Fri–Sat 11–10, Sun 11–9 ⊛

ESTRELLA NEGRA $ / ★★★
2346 W. Fullerton (Western), Bucktown
Mexican/Brunch
Owner Otoniel Michel envisioned a place where art, music, Mexican food, friends, and family could all intersect in one place. Estrella Negra hits on all points. After being greeted by the original mural on the side of the building (produced by a friend of the owner's), you know you're entering a unique space. Locally produced Mexican art populates the walls and tables (which are for sale), and local musicians and artists perform on weekends in the front window. Michel's mother whips up chicken *pozole* and other traditional dishes, their creative presentation adding to the restaurant's visual interest. The menu includes nonalcoholic piña colada, margarita, mango, and strawberry mixes—you bring the rum or tequila. A lower-level private party room accommodates 25.
(773) 227-5993, estrellanegra.com, Mon closed, Tues–Thurs 5–10:30, Fri–Sat 5–1 ⚓ ⚘

ETHAN'S CAFÉ $$ / ★
2201 N. Sheffield (Webster), Lincoln Park
Japanese/Korean

This casual sushi BYOB is great for a quick bite in the DePaul neighborhood. Ethan's caters to the student population with coffee drinks, a smoothie bar, all-you-can-eat specials, and a few Korean and Japanese dishes from the kitchen as alternatives to the more expensive maki rolls. If you haven't eaten here before, make sure you inquire about their policies regarding minimum orders and leftover charges.

(773) 244-9012, Mon–Thurs 10–10, Fri 10–11, Sat 11–11, Sun closed 🦐 🏖

EVERYDAY THAI $ / ★★
1509 W. Devon (Greenview), Edgewater
Thai

Noiy Ruttanamongkongul and Suthamas Petiwat took over this 24-seat spot in 2008 which, like so many other Asian BYOBs, focuses on takeout and delivery service. The owners, who also double as chefs, use authentic spices and ingredients. The results are more intensely flavored curries and lots of heat in dishes such as the seafood with chili and basil leaf.

(773) 262-7797, everydaythaionline.com, Wed–Mon 12–10, Tues closed ⊗

FATTOUSH $$$ / ★★
2652 N. Halsted (Wrightwood), Lincoln Park
Middle Eastern

Named after a traditional Lebanese salad (made with romaine, tomatoes, cucumbers, parsley, mint, sumac, onions, peppers, garlic, olive oil, and lemon), Fattoush strives for affordable, authentic Lebanese cuisine in a casual environment. They will chill your bottles in the fridge on request.

(773) 327-2652, fattoushrestaurant.com, Mon 12–10, Tues closed, Wed–Thurs 12–9, Fri–Sat 12–10, Sun 12–8 ⊗

FEED $$ / ★
2803 W. Chicago (California), Humboldt Park
American/Brunch
The flashing electric Jesus and other kitschy items have vanished,
victims of a recent remodeling, but the down-home vibe and
comfort-food menu remain. Diners order sandwiches (pulled
pork, fried catfish), sides (okra, mac and cheese) and, of course,
chicken—all served cafeteria style. Nightly specials include steak,
pork chops, and gumbo. Cash only.
(773) 489-4600, feedrestaurantchicago.com, Mon–Fri 8–10, Sat
9–10, Sun 9–9 ⊗ 🏴 💵

5 LOAVES EATERY $$ / ★★
405 E. 75th (S. King Dr.), South Side
American/Brunch
Breakfast is the specialty at this Park Manor neighborhood place
on the South Side, which caters to the morning crowd with a
variety of breakfast platters, sandwiches, and à la carte items.
For BYOB diners, there's a dinner menu that ranges from spinach
salad to salmon croquettes ("with a spicy twist") and catfish po'
boys. Live jazz is featured every first Friday of the month.
(773) 873-6666, Mon closed, Tues–Wed 8–7, Thurs–Sat 8–8, Sun
8–7 ⊗ Ⓟ

FLYING CHICKEN $$ / ★★
3402 W. Montrose (Kimball), Albany Park
Colombian
After several years on Lincoln Avenue, Flying Chicken (also
known as *pollo volador*) moved to Albany Park and is staying
BYOB "for now." The atmosphere is informal, without being
hole-in-the-wall, and specialties include *pollo a la brasa*, or roasted
chicken, and grilled steak. There are also a few seafood options,
and a side order of fried plantains will satisfy your sweet tooth.
(773) 463-0228, Mon–Fri 11–10, Sat 11–11, Sun 12–9 ⊗

FLYING SAUCER $ / ★
1123 N. California (Haddon), Humboldt Park
Eclectic/Brunch
Flying Saucer has evolved into a reliable breakfast and lunch
diner where organic ingredients, tofu, and veggies dominate
the menu (flying tofu bowl, fried chicken, veggie lentil burger,
huevos volando, tofu and sweet potato hash). BYOB was a lot more
popular here when Flying Saucer used to serve dinner, but your
bottle of beer, wine, or Champagne is still welcome, especially
during weekend brunch.
(773) 342-9076, 8–3 daily ✪ 💲

FOGATA VILLAGE $$ / ★★
1820 S. Ashland (18th), Pilsen
Mexican/Brunch
This café-like spot, with exposed brick walls and high ceilings, is
the creation of chef/owner Agustin Bahena, a protégé of Columbia
and Chicago Yacht Clubs. A smattering of Italian dishes invades
the otherwise Mexican menu, and the shrimp options read like a
scene from *Forrest Gump*: spicy garlic, *à la diabla*, fajitas, Jamaican,
chipotle, *à la suiza*—the list goes on. Karaoke livens up the place
on weekends.
(312) 850-1702, fogatavillage.com, Sun–Wed 8–9, Thurs–Sat
8–10:30 ✪

GALAPAGOS CAFÉ $$ / ★★
3213 W. Irving Park (Kedzie), Albany Park
Ecuadorian/Japanese
A sushi and Ecuadorian menu seems like a strange concept (not
to mention the restaurant's name), but regulars here seem to
make it work. Most order appetizers from the sushi/maki side,
followed by an Ecuadorian entrée. Traditional Ecuadorian dishes,
distinguished by marinated, not sauced, meats, include the
pescado encocado (fish with coconut milk, onions, green peppers,
tomatoes, and plantains) and *mote pillo* (corn with eggs, onions,
and herbs). The hodgepodge of wall hangings complements the
menu's quirkiness.
(773) 754-8265, Sun–Thurs 10–10, Fri–Sat 10–11 ✪ Ⓟ

GARLIC & CHILI $ / ★
1232 N. LaSalle (Scott), Old Town
Thai

This ultra-casual neighborhood Thai place (same owner as Thai Classic, a BYOB in Lakeview) focuses on takeout and delivery service, so a liquor license was never in the business plan. But BYOB is encouraged, so tote a six-pack of Singha or bottle of Pinot Gris to accompany your meal of traditional Thai fare. There are several good wine stores nearby (see "Wine & Spirits Stores A–Z" for locations).

(312) 255-1717, Mon–Sat 11:30–9:30, Sun closed ⊛

GAUDI COFFEE AND GRILL $$ / ★★
624 N. Ashland (Erie), West Town
Spanish/Brunch

Sisters Betty and Veronica Romo (is there an Archie in the family?) have done wonders with this small space. Mosaics and local art don the walls, and the menu is a long list of tapas, or small plates of Spanish cuisine, such as rib eye over toasted bread with melted blue cheese and grilled calamari. They carry freshly made nonalcoholic sangria and margarita mixes (why don't more BYOBs do this?). On Sundays a flamenco guitarist serenades the brunch crowd.

(312) 733-9528, gaudicoffeegrill.com, 8–10 daily ⚲ ⚑

GINO'S EAST $ / ★
2801 N. Lincoln (Diversey), Lakeview
Italian

Deep dish pizza is the specialty at this small neighborhood joint (the only Gino's East that's BYOB). Choose from spinach, cheese, four-meat, supreme, or vegetarian options. There are also thin-crust 'zas, stromboli (a strudel-like pizza), pastas, sandwiches, and salads. The best deal is the 9-inch personal deep dish pizza, which is only about five bucks.

(773) 327-3737, ginoseast.com, Mon–Thurs 11–10:30, Fri–Sat 11–12, Sun 12–10:30 ⊛ ⚑ Ⓟ

GIO'S CAFÉ & DELI $$ / ★★
2724 S. Lowe (28th), Bridgeport
Italian

The word is out about this neighborhood gem, led by Giovanni
Liuzzo ("Nacho") and Ignacio Bautista (Rosebud, Bella Note).
What started as a deli and retail store carrying authentic Southern
Italian foods has blossomed into a 50-seat café serving homemade
pastas, entrées, and desserts.
(312) 225-6368, gioscafe.com, Mon–Sat 10–9, Sun closed ✵

GLORIA'S CAFÉ $$ / ★★
3300 W. Fullerton (Spaulding), Logan Square
Colombian

In Colombia, rotisserie chicken (*pollo a la brasa*) is one of the
most popular dishes. While owners Gloria and Jaime Santiago
offer several different variations on this dish, they also offer a full
array of other Colombian cuisine, from grilled steaks and shrimp
entrées to sides such as Colombian sausage, fried cassava, and
sweet fried plantains. The staff can scrounge up a few wine glasses
and a corkscrew on request.
(773) 342-1050, Mon–Thurs 9–8, Fri–Sat 9–9, Sun 10–6 ⊗

GOLDEN BULL $$ / -
242 W. Cermak (Wentworth), Chinatown
Chinese

This long-standing eatery offers Americanized Chinese fare (egg
rolls, sweet and sour pork, fried rice, egg foo yong, chop suey).
There's also a separate Chinese menu for more authentic options.
They tend to change their hours at whim, but can always be
counted on to stay open late.
(312) 808-1668, Sat–Mon 12–1a, Tues–Fri 3–1a ⊗

GOLDEN THAI $ / ★★
1509 W. Taylor (Laflin), University Village/Little Italy
Thai

Who knew this block of Taylor Street was such a mecca for ethnic
BYOBs? This charming spot offers the usual array of Thai noodle
and fried rice dishes, but the real highlights are the 15 or so "stir-
fried and steamed" options, like lime chicken, pepper beef, BBQ
pork, garlic chicken, roasted duck, and others.
(312) 733-0760, Mon–Fri 11–10, Sat–Sun 12–10 ⊗

GRAND KATACHI $$$ / ★★
4747 N. Damen (Lawrence), Ravenswood
Japanese

The owners of Katachi (a Lakeview BYOB) split; one stayed and changed the name to Oh Fusion, the other moved to this location, the former site of a Moroccan restaurant. The "red price" promotion, which was available only during happy hour, has now been incorporated into the regular menu. And because there's a liquor license moratorium on this block, Grand Katachi is BYOB indefinitely. BYOB *and* happy hour deals? Quite the stimulus package. (773) 271-4541, grandkatachi.com, Sun–Thurs 5–10, Fri–Sat 5–11 🍷

GRANDE NOODLES & SUSHI BAR $–$$$ / ★★
6632 N. Clark (Wallen), Rogers Park
Japanese/Thai

If you need to please both Thai and sushi fans in your group, this is the place. Grande serves a full menu of both cuisines, including banana duck curry and *moo ping* (grilled pork) from the Thai side and orange maki (fried red snapper, cream cheese, masago) and traditional sushi from the other. (773) 761-6666, Mon–Thurs 11:30–9:30, Fri–Sat 11:30–10, Sun 12–9:30 🍷

GRAPE LEAVES $ / ★★
129 S. Oak Park Avenue (South Blvd.), Oak Park
Middle Eastern

If the downtown Oak Park eateries are packed, try this out-of-the-way place for a cheap, tasty bite. All the Middle Eastern standards are here: falafel, kebabs, shawerma, hummus, tabouleh, and the eponymous dish, stuffed with rice, raisins, and almonds. Go early on the weekends or make a reservation; the cozy dining room seats only about 20. (708) 848-5555, grapeleaves.us, 11:30–10 daily 🍷

GREEK CORNER $$ / ★
958 N. Damen (Augusta), Ukrainian Village
Greek
In business for nearly 20 years, this corner diner is testament to
the neighborhood's preference for solid, family-owned, ethnic eateries. Find traditional Greek faves such as souvlaki, Greek salad,
pastitsio (ground meat layered with pasta, cheese, and white
sauce), moussaka, and Greek pizzas on pita bread. A charming
outdoor patio is open in the summer.
(773) 252-8010, Mon–Sat 11:30–10, Sun closed ✎ ⋗

THE GROCERY BISTRO $$$ / ★★★
804 W. Washington (Halsted), West Loop
Contemporary American
Chef-driven BYOBs don't come along very often, nor are there
many near the downtown area. But the Grocery Bistro is not in
any hurry to get its liquor license, so this culinary gem looks like
it's here to stay (having a boutique wine shop next door doesn't
hurt). The menu is an eclectic mix of contemporary American
"shared plates" and entrées, made with seasonal ingredients
sourced at local markets. The communal table accommodates
large parties, and the beverage service is top-notch. Watch out for
the steep corkage fee, though.
(312) 850-9291, thegrocerybistro.com, Mon–Thurs 5–11, Fri–Sat
5–12, Sun closed, reservations recommended ✎ ⋗

HABANA LIBRE $$ / ★★
1440 W. Chicago (Bishop), West Town
Cuban
This cozy, friendly neighborhood eatery had applied for its liquor
license when the last edition of this book went to press. The
good/bad news is that the license was not approved, but they're
still in business and still cranking out great, homemade Cuban
food. The veggie empanadas, red snapper, and fried plantains are
all highlights. (Did I mention how cozy and friendly this place is?)
(312) 243-3303, Mon–Thurs 11–9:30, Fri–Sat 11–10,
Sun 12–9 ✎

HABIBI $$ / ★★
1225–27 W. Devon (Clark), Rogers Park
Middle Eastern

I'm sure that this independently owned Lebanese restaurant on the North Side didn't plan on having anything in common with McDonald's and Starbucks by being open 365 days a year. But rest assured that the comparisons with franchises and fast food stop there. Open since spring 2009, Habibi offers a wide variety of made-to-order Middle Eastern dishes in a casual atmosphere. (773) 465-9318, Sun–Thurs 11–10:30, Fri–Sat 11–12 ⚞

HALINA'S POLISH DELIGHTS $$ / ★★
5914 W. Lawrence (Austin), Northwest Side
Polish

This is one of those places that didn't know it was BYOB until the foodie population christened it so. Since 1994, owner and cook Halina (first name only, like Cher), has been serving up heaping plates of made-to-order Polish grub like pierogi (up to 12 varieties on any given day) and Polish sausage in a 40-seat, homey dining room. The budget- and belt-busting "Polish Plate" is a sampler of pork chops, sausage, pierogi, and sides. At only $10.95, it should sustain you until payday.
(773) 205-0256, 12–9 daily ⊛

HAMAMATSU $$$ / ★★
5143 N. Clark (Foster), Uptown
Japanese

Sushi is the main attraction at this traditional Japanese spot. But Hamamatsu also offers a few Korean dishes, such as *bibim-bob* and kimchee tofu, and Japanese items from the kitchen, like katsu, a Japanese-style cutlet of pork, beef, fish, or chicken, deep-fried in light-as-air breading. Wine glasses and corkscrews are available on request.
(773) 506-2978, hamamatsuchicago.com, Mon–Thurs 4–10, Fri 4–11, Sat 12–11, Sun 12–10 ⚞

HASHALOM RESTAURANT $ / ★★
2905 W. Devon (Francisco), West Rogers Park
Israeli/Moroccan

Jacques Zrihen has been serving extremely affordable authentic
Israeli and Moroccan cuisine to the neighborhood since the
mid-1980s. There are many reasons to come here besides the
prices—homemade falafel, shish kebabs, and *bourekas*, to name a
few. But this may be the only place in town that makes *shakshou-
ka*, a popular Israeli dish made with eggs, tomatoes, and peppers.
Call ahead and order the vegetarian or meat couscous (available
on Fridays and Saturdays only); it has a six-hour prep time.
(773) 465-5675, Mon–Tues closed, Wed–Sun 12–9 ⊕ ⊡

HATSU HANA $$$ / ★★★
3136 N. Broadway (Briar), Lakeview
Japanese

This isn't your standard all-you-can-eat Lakeview sushi joint.
Trained sushi chefs create sophisticated appetizers (sashimi
carpaccio, tuna taki, seared scallop) and beautiful specialty rolls,
like the green turtle, summer, and super white dragon. (They
applied for a liquor license a long time ago; call ahead to make
sure they're still BYOB.)
(773) 528-1902, Mon–Thurs 11:30–10, Fri 11:30–11, Sat–Sun
12–11 ⊕

HB HOME BISTRO $$$ / ★★★
3403 N. Halsted (Roscoe), Lakeview
Contemporary American

Chef/owner Joncarl Lachman's bistro is one of the best-loved
BYOBs in the city. Serving classic bistro food, Lachman uses
locally sourced and organic ingredients for an eclectic menu that
features at least three nightly specials based on his "whimsy and
what's available at the market." Expect dishes like the HB lamb
burger (on toasted pretzel roll with brie and a side of truffle fries),
baked grouper nicoise, and almond-stuffed dates—not to mention
the incredible homemade desserts. Lachman plays homage to his
Dutch heritage by recreating *gezellig,* or a candlelit atmosphere
enjoyed all hours of the day, and menu items such as Amsterdam
mussels and *shert*, a split pea soup with sausage and caraway.
(773) 661-0299, homebistrochicago.com, Mon–Tues closed,
Wed–Thurs 5–10, Fri–Sat 5–10:30, Sun 5–9, reservations
recommended ⊕

HEALTHY FOOD LITHUANIAN RESTAURANT $$ / ★★

3236 S. Halsted (32nd), Bridgeport
American/Lithuanian

Owner Gina Biciunas-Santoski's parents bought this place in 1960, when she was just a freshman in high school. She took over 30 years ago, maintaining the restaurant's traditional Lithuanian menu (cold beet soup, stuffed cabbage, Lithuanian pancakes) and original decor ("people tell me things haven't changed in years"). While the popular *kugelis* (potatoes, eggs, onions, bacon, and sour cream) may not bring the word "healthy" to mind, Healthy Food Lithuanian's concept is based on the philosophy that food should never be made from processed ingredients. Gina travels miles to source authentic cheeses, handpicks her own blueberries for the homemade dumplings—whatever needs to be done to preserve this philosophy. Be sure to congratulate her on making the Senior Olympics swim team (offering a sip of your wine will do).
(312) 326-2724, healthyfoodlithuanian-chicago.com, Mon closed, Tues–Wed 8–4, Thurs–Sat 8–8, Sun 8–5 ⊛ 💲 ATM

HEMA'S KITCHEN $$ / ★★

2439 W. Devon (Artesian), West Rogers Park
Indian

After almost 20 years of serving regulars at the cramped location around the corner, local legend and chef/owner Hema Potla opened this larger space—and capacity crowds followed in no time. The menu is slightly different at this location; you'll find almost a dozen different types of homemade breads and several of "Hema's Sizzlers," or the chef's favorites (*paneer tikka, lamb boti kebob, murg malai tikka*).
(773) 338-1627, hemaskitchen.net, 11–11 daily ⊛

HEMA'S KITCHEN II $$ / ★★

2411 N. Clark (Fullerton), Lincoln Park
Indian

This Lincoln Park offspring offers nearly 75 entrées, evenly split between vegetarian and meat options (lamb, chicken, or sea-food). Local liquor stores carry several Indian beers (Taj Mahal, etc.), though a decent IPA or Riesling proves a better pairing for Indian cuisine.
(773) 529-1705, hemaskitchen.net, 12–11 daily ⊛

HING KEE $ / ★
2140 S. Archer (Cermak), Chinatown
Pan-Asian
New owners recently took over this place, which is located in
Chinatown Square. They kept the name and affordable prices, but
made radical changes to the dining room and expanded upstairs
with a 120-seat dining area that serves double duty as a private
party room. The chef here specializes in *chiu chow*–style cooking,
though the Asian menu casts its net far and wide, trapping Thai,
Japanese, Chinese, and Vietnamese dishes like the fresh mushroom and baked eel with fried rice.
(312) 808-9538, chinatownhingkee.com, 10–12 daily ⊗ ♥

HIRO'S CAFÉ $$ / ★★
2936 N. Broadway (Oakdale), Lakeview
Japanese/Korean
In Koryo's former space (the awning is still there, providing some
confusion), the new owner has retained a few of the Korean menu
items Koryo offered (*bee-bim bop, chop chae, bulgogi*) and added
some à la carte Japanese dishes (udon, sushi, maki). There's also
a daily all-you-can-eat sushi buffet from 5–10 for under $20.
Liquor license pending (but a corkage fee will not be charged if
it's approved).
(773) 477-8510, Mon–Thurs 5–11, Fri–Sun 5–12 ⊗

HOANH LONG $$ / ★★
6144 N. Lincoln (McCormick), Lincolnwood
Vietnamese
Vietnamese dining options are few and far between in Chicagoland, especially outside of Uptown. Hoanh Long ("strong
dragon") is such a welcome addition to the area that customers are willing to brave limited parking and hole-in-the-wall
atmosphere to feast on the homemade *pho*, marinated beef with
vegetables, steamed rice noodle *bún*, and hot pots.
(773) 583-7770, Mon closed, Tues–Thurs 10:30–10, Fri–Sat
10–10:30, Sun 10–10, reservations recommended on weekends ⊗

HONEY 1 BBQ $$ / ★
2241 N. Western (Lyndale), Bucktown
BBQ

On certain days you can smell Honey 1's hickory-filled smoker
while driving down this block of Western. Owner Robert Adams
uses a dry rub on his prized slabs of ribs, sausages, rib tips, pulled
pork, and chicken then slow-smokes them in a glassed-in smoker
in true Arkansas BBQ fashion. Corkscrews and plastic cups are
available (the focus is on the food, not BYOB).
(773) 227-5130, honey1bbq.com, Mon closed, Tues–Thurs
11–9:30, Fri–Sat 11–11 ⊛

HONKY TONK BBQ $$ / ★★
1213 W. 18th (12th), Pilsen
BBQ

Memphis-style ribs, chicken, brisket, sausage, and pulled pork are
dry-rubbed then slow-cooked in the on-site applewood smoker
(which operates off the grid!) for 16 hours before diners devour
them with homemade sauce. Honky Tonk's pork shoulder won
third place at the 2008 Memphis in May International Festival, a
major upset to established competitors. Come see what the fuss
is all about—and rock out to country swing bands Thursday
through Saturday nights.
(312) 226-7427, honkytonkbbqchicago.com, Sun–Mon closed,
Tues–Sat 4–9:30 ⚑ 🖃

HOT DOUG'S $ / ★
3324 N. California (Roscoe), Irving Park
Eclectic

I used to work with Doug Sohn, a.k.a. "Hot Doug," and he would
dream about owning "an encased meat emporium." Sounded like
a bizarre plan at the time, but the laugh's on anyone who, well,
actually laughed. Sohn holds court at this gourmet sausage joint,
chatting up and serving anywhere from 200–700 addicts daily. As
you're waiting in the block-long line, check the Web site for the
daily specials, which range from bacon and elk cheddar sausage
to blue cheese pork sausage with crème fraiche and almonds
(vegetarian and chicken sausage options always available). Offers
of fine wine to the host accepted.
(773) 279-9550, hotdougs.com, Mon–Sat 10:30–4, Sun
closed ⊛ 🏴

HOT WOKS, COOL SUSHI $$ / ★★
3930 N. Pulaski (Irving Park), Irving Park
Pan-Asian
More and more contemporary eateries like this cute, Asian/sushi
hybrid seem to be popping up on the Northwest Side. Seating is a
little tight, but there's a roomy second floor to accommodate larger
parties. The owners (My Thai) have developed a Pan-Asian "greatest hits" menu that includes sushi and maki. It's worth the trip just
to read the description for the Obama-nami signature roll.
(773) 282-1818, hotwokscoolsushi.com, Sun–Thurs 11:30–9,
Fri–Sat 11:30–10 ⊛ ⤙ Ⓟ

I MONELLI TRATTORIA PIZZERIA $$ / ★★
5019 N. Western (Winnemac), Lincoln Square
Italian
Giovanni Carzedda (Il Covo) and partners Marco Schiavoni and
Massimiliano Agostino (Pizza Metro on Ashland) are behind this
casual neighborhood place, which features simple Italian fare at
budget-friendly prices. Start out with one of their antipasti or
salads, then move on to the Roma-style square pizzas, paninis,
pastas, or monthly specials.
(773) 561-8499, http://imonelli.info, Mon 3–10, Tues closed, Wed
3–10, Thurs 11–10, Fri–Sat 11–11, Sun 11–10 ⤙ ⤙

ICOSIUM KAFÉ $ / ★★
5200 N. Clark (Foster), Andersonville
Algerian/Brunch
Bel Elmetennani (Mamacita's, Icosium in Lincoln Park) strikes
again with this cute neighborhood spot, specializing in Algerian
crepes. Try them for breakfast (apricot jam and brie; eggs, ricotta,
and merguez), savory varieties for dinner, and of course sweet
crepes for dessert (Belgian chocolate and berries, mango and
gingery chutney). All meat served is halal.
(773) 271-5233, icosiumkafe.com, Mon–Fri 9–10, Sat–Sun
8–10 ⊛

THE INDIA GRILL $$ / ★★
1112 S. Wabash (11th), South Loop
Indian
The *biryani*, a basmati rice dish cooked with lamb, chicken, seafood, or vegetables, has put this bi-level, 200-seat Northern Indian place on the South Loop map. Open since fall 2008, The India Grill also offers cuisine from the tandoor, a clay oven used to roast the popular tandoori chicken and bake naan (bread). Lunch and dinner buffets are served from 12–3 and 5–10, respectively. Or order from the menu of traditional Indian vegetarian and meat-based appetizers and entrées.
(312) 662-1111, theindiagrill.com, 12–3, 5–10 daily ⊛

INDIAN GRILL $$ / ★★★
2258 N. Clark (Belden), Lincoln Park
Indian
Owner Ram Sharma initially opened this Northern Indian restaurant without a liquor license, but when his application was finally approved he lost so many BYOB customers that he went back to being a BYOB. That was several years ago; today customers can enjoy tandoori specialties, vindaloo, *matar paneer*, and samosas with their store-bought beer or wine in an elegant, contemporary setting.
(773) 477-8000, indiangrillrestaurants.com, Mon–Wed 5–10, Thurs 11:30–3, 5–10, Fri–Sat 11:30–10:30, Sun 11:30–3, 5–10 ⊛

INDIE CAFÉ $$$ / ★★★
5951 N. Broadway (Thorndale), Rogers Park
Japanese/Thai
The hip, contemporary decor (think Chiasso meets CB2) and throngs of young professionals make for a popular spot on weekends. The signature maki presentations are phenomenal, especially the crocodile (made with an entire eel), fire komodo, and white scorpion. They provide full beverage service.
(773) 561-5577, indiecafe.us, Mon–Thurs 11:30–10, Fri–Sat 11:30–10:30, Sun 12–10, reservations recommended on weekends ⊛

IRAZU $$ / ★
1865 N. Milwaukee (Oakley), Wicker Park
Costa Rican

After nearly 20 years in business, Irazu's exploding popularity mandated some light remodeling and additional outdoor seating with an enclosed patio. The only Costa Rican BYOB in the city, Irazu's menu is straight-up Costa Rican cuisine, which means lots of beans and rice and tropical fruits and vegetables. There's a communal cooler to chill your bottles in the summer.
(773) 252-5687, irazuchicago.com, Mon–Sat 11:30–9:30, Sun closed ✂ 🐟 💵 ATM

ISLA PILIPINA $ / ★★
2501 W. Lawrence (Campbell), Ravenswood
Philippine

New management took over this casual place that boasts authentic cuisine from the Philippines. The specialties are *pancit bihon* (pan-fried noodles with chicken, pork, and veggies) and their award-winning mixed adobo, a dish made with chicken and pork in a garlic, vinegar, and pepper sauce. Why are they BYOB? "Our culture tends to drink," says an undisclosed staff member, "so we opted to not get our liquor license to prevent any problems." There's a liquor store a few doors down, in the same shopping plaza.
(773) 271-2988, islapilipina.com, Mon closed, Tues–Sat 11–9, Sun 11–7 ⊛ Ⓟ

ISTANBUL RESTAURANT $$ / ★★
3613 N. Broadway (Addison), Lakeview
Turkish/Brunch

Yasar Demir (Café Demir, Fast and Fresh) offers breakfast, dinner, and weekend brunch at this 85-seat eatery, his most ambitious undertaking to date. The menu is mostly traditional Turkish cuisine, but a few American dishes (steaks, salmon) are available for the uninitiated. Breads and *pideh* (Turkish pies) are baked on-site. Free parking is available in North Community Bank's lot weekdays after 6 p.m. and all weekend.
(773) 525-0500, 7–11 daily ⊛ Ⓟ

JAI-YEN FUSION RESTAURANT $–$$$ / ★★★
3736 N. Broadway (Grace), Lakeview
Japanese/Thai

Don't let the word "fusion" mislead you: there are separate Japanese and Thai menus, not one that combines the two cuisines. Semantics aside, Jai-Yen (Thai for "be patient, relax") is a tranquil space with a Japanese-inspired decor in Genesee Depot's old spot. The maki rolls are high on presentation, so expect complex, multi-layered creations. There are also several Thai soups, apps, and noodle and rice dishes. Sake cups and sake pitchers are available on request.
(773) 404-0555, jai-yen.com, Sun–Thurs 11:30–10:30, Fri–Sat 11:30–11 ⊛

JASMINE RICE $ / ★★
3103 N. Narragansett (Barry), Northwest Side
Japanese/Thai

This neighborhood Thai joint is located within 100 feet of a school *and* a church, so its BYOB status is practically guaranteed. In an area teeming with Mexican, Chinese, and Italian takeout, Jasmine Rice's Thai and Japanese menu offers a refreshing change of pace. Owners took special care with the decor; hand-painted lithos and other items were shipped from Thailand to add an authentic touch.
(773) 836-1288, 11–10 daily ⊛

JIM NOODLE & RICE $ / -
2819 N. Lincoln (Diversey), Lakeview
Thai

The focus here is on takeout and delivery service, which should be fairly obvious once you stumble into the tiny, 12-seat dining area that's wedged next to the open grill. However, a charming outdoor garden patio in back accommodates 16 in warmer months. Vegetarians can choose from almost 30 entrées. Beverage service? You're on your own.
(773) 935-5912, jimnoodle.com, Mon–Sat 11:30–10, Sun 4–10 ⊛ ⚑

JITLADA THAI HOUSE $ / ★★
3715 N. Halsted (Grace), Lakeview
Thai
New owners took over this space recently and remodeled with a
blue and green color scheme, which gives the room a Caribbean-
like feel. The menu is still a greatest hits selection of Thai apps,
salads, soups, curries, and noodle and rice dishes, with more
emphasis on presentation.
(773) 388-9988, 11:30–11:30 daily ⊛

JOSE'S RESTAURANT $$ / ★★★★
806 N. Winchester (Chicago), East Ukrainian Village
Mexican
Jose Hernandez, Jr., runs this charming eatery, located in the back
of Rio Balsas Market. Feel like a margarita? They sell freshly made
nonalcoholic margarita mix, served in jumbo margarita glasses
with rim salt and lime. Just bring the tequila. Jose carries a huge
selection of Champagne flutes, martini glasses, cocktail shakers,
wine glasses, and pilsner glasses, so the sky's the limit when
choosing your poison for the evening.
(773) 269-3188, Mon closed, Tues–Fri 10–11, Sat–Sun 9–11 ⚑

JOY YEE NOODLE $ / ★
521 Davis (Chicago), Evanston
Pan-Asian
Joy Yee's offers updated versions of Thai, Korean, Chinese, and
Vietnamese dishes. They have become increasingly popular
throughout the city and, now, the suburbs. Rather than a fusion
approach, there are separate menus for all four cuisines. If you
can't decide what to order, the "food art" in the window may help
you choose. All locations provide water glasses and corkscrews.
(847) 733-1900, joyyee.com, Mon–Thurs 11:30–9, Fri–Sat
11:30–10, Sun 12–9 ⊛ ⚑

JOY YEE NOODLE $ / ★
2139–41 South China Pl. (Cermak), Chinatown
Pan-Asian
(312) 328-0001, 11–10:30 daily ⊛ ♈

JOY YEE NOODLE $ / ★
1335 S. Halsted (Maxwell), University Village/Little Italy
Pan-Asian
(312) 997-2128, Mon–Thurs 11–10, Fri–Sat 11:30–10:30, Sun
12–10 ⊛

JOY YEE NOODLE $ / ★
1163 E. Ogden (Iroquois), Naperville
Pan-Asian
(630) 579-6800, Mon–Thurs 11:30–9, Fri–Sat 11:30–10, Sun
12–9 ⊛

JOY YEE PLUS $$$ / ★
2159 S. China Place (Cermak), Chinatown
Japanese/Vietnamese
Not content with just one location in the neighborhood, owners
opened Joy Yee Plus, which only offers two cuisines: Japanese and
Vietnamese. If you encounter a gaper's block at the entrance, it's
due to the entrancing koi pond installed in the acrylic floor. Glass
tile and bright, modern touches amp up the contemporary atmosphere. A private party room upstairs accommodates about 60.
(312) 328-0001, 11–10:30 daily ⊛ ♈

JOY'S NOODLES & RICE $ / ★★
3257 N. Broadway (Aldine), Lakeview
Thai
Joy's has become synonymous with Lakeview and Boystown, serving locals a basic Thai menu of noodles, rice dishes, and curries
for over 20 years. The large, airy space, with exposed brick walls
and warm neutral tones, offers a relaxing environment, and there's
a roomy outdoor patio in the back that's removed from noisy
Broadway. The owners also run Noodles in the Pot, a BYOB in
Lincoln Park that serves the same menu.
(773) 327-8330, Sun–Thurs 11–10, Fri–Sat 11–11 ⊛ ⚑

KAN ZAMAN $$$ / ★★★★
617 N. Wells (Ohio), River North
Middle Eastern
This place serves authentic Lebanese cuisine, which features
marinated, subtly seasoned meats and lots of garlic and olive oil.
The tender filet mignon kebabs are the most popular dish. Since
they had a liquor license way back when (and may soon again),
Kan Zaman carries just about any type of glassware you need—
from cordial glasses to red and white wine stemware to chilled
beer mugs.
(312) 751-9600, kanzamanchicago.com, Mon–Thurs 11–10,
Fri 11–12, Sat 12–12, Sun 3–10, reservations recommended on
weekends 🕯 🍹

KANOK $$ / ★★
3422 N. Broadway (Hawthorne), Lakeview
Pan-Asian
Formerly Ecce Café, this space was redecorated with sleek,
modern Asian accents, and Korean, Chinese, and Thai items
were added to the sushi menu. Owners dropped the oddball
brunch and lunch menus (Korean burgers anyone?) but kept the
tried-and-true maki and sushi selections. There are also several
sushi platters, Chinese and Thai noodle and rice dishes, and
over a dozen entrées to choose from, from kung pao chicken to
beef teriyaki.
(773) 529-2525, 4–10 daily 🍴

KAPEEKOO $ / ★★
6336 S. Pulaski (63rd), South Side
Caribbean
Chef/owner Esmerelda Melendez was highly influenced by
two things: her Puerto Rican mother's cooking and a game of
dominoes ("kapeekoo" is a term used for this old Puerto Rican
pastime). Melendez's casual West Lawn eatery takes a modern
spin on Caribbean-inspired cuisine. Choose from the *jibarito*
sandwich, Jamaican jerk chicken, stuffed tamales, and more.
(773) 284-9400, kapeekoo.com, Mon closed, Tues–Thurs 11–9,
Fri 11–10, Sat 12:30–10, Sun 12:30–9 🍴

KARYN'S FRESH CORNER CAFÉ $$ / ★★★
1901 N. Halsted (Armitage), Lincoln Park
Vegetarian/Brunch
Karyn's Fresh Corner has become a veritable emporium for raw food enthusiasts. Next to the raw café and juice bar, inner beauty center, and store is this beautiful gourmet restaurant, which serves raw cuisine for lunch, dinner, and an all-you-can-eat $29.95 weekend brunch. Reasonably priced dinner options include raw versions of pad Thai, falafel, ravioli, pizza, tamales, soups, and several desserts. Wine glasses, Champagne flutes, ice buckets, and corkscrews are available on request.
(312) 255-1590, karynraw.com, 11:30–10 daily, Sun brunch 11:30–3:30 ✦ 🍴 Ⓟ

KEN-KEE $ / -
2129A S. China Place, Chinatown
Chinese
Liquor licenses are hard to come by in this area, so the majority of the small noodle shops and cafés are BYOB. After strolling through Chinatown Square's curious shops and bakeries, stop at this casual spot for Hong Kong–style cuisine, like the ken-kee special (with squid, chicken, or pork skin), congee (rice soup), or vegetables with pork. BYO bottle opener.
(312) 326-2088, 11–1a daily 🐟

KIKUYA $$$ / ★★★
1601 E. 55th (Lake Park), Hyde Park
Japanese
One of the more established eateries in the U of C area, Kikuya's menu and decor reflect traditional Japanese influences, rather than the modern sushi/Asian eateries that have mushroomed all over Chicagoland. The menu offers Japanese staples—sushi, tempura, udon, katsu—in simple, classic surroundings.
(773) 667-3727, kikuyaonline.com, Mon 4–9:30, Tues–Sun 11:30–9:30, reservations recommended on weekends 🐟

KIN SUSHI AND THAI $$ / ★★★
1134 N. Milwaukee (Haddon), Noble Square
Japanese/Thai

Former Tsunami and Tiparos chefs banded together and opened Kin ("eat" in Thai, "gold" in Japanese), a modern sushi bar and Thai restaurant. Capitalizing on the BYOB trend, they have no plans to apply for a liquor license anytime soon. The space is especially charming at night, when the soft glow of candles softens the dark walls and stark atmosphere. They provide full beverage service upon request, including sake cups.
(773) 772-2722, kinchicago.com, Mon–Thurs 11–10, Fri–Sat 11–11, Sun 4–10 ✪

KING OF THAI $ / ★★
1129 W. Argyle (Broadway), Uptown
Thai

One of the many newer restaurants on this block, this cute, contemporary-looking Thai eatery seems—at first blush—that it would be more at home in Lincoln Park than Uptown. Happily, there are plenty of authentic Thai dishes (*yen ta four*, *kuwy juub*, fish maw soup) to remind you that you're on Argyle Street. Regulars sing the praises of tom yum noodles (a broth of pork, Chinese greens, bean sprouts, meatballs, peanuts, and wontons served over rice), roast duck noodles (BBQ duck and Chinese greens served over egg noodles), and others that Thai joints typically hide in a "secret menu."
(773) 784-7777, Fri–Wed 11–9:30, Thurs closed ✪

KITCHENETTE $–$$$ / ★★
3811 N. Ashland (Grace), Lakeview
Japanese/Thai

The owners of Mr. Thai changed the name, added sushi to the menu, and spruced up the dining room with a fresh coat of pumpkin-colored paint and new lighting fixtures. The result is a brighter, more modern-looking space. The Thai side of the menu hasn't changed much, but now the kitchen cranks out a few Japanese dishes (tempura, katsu), and several maki, temaki, and entrée/à la carte sushi options are available from the new sushi bar.
(773) 244-9300, Mon–Fri 11:30–10, Sat–Sun 12–10 ✪

KNEW $$$$ / ★★★★
2556 W. Fullerton (Rockwell), Logan Square
Eclectic
Chef/co-owner Omar Rodriquez's second restaurant is just down
the street from his first fine-dining BYOB, Think, which closed in
summer 2009. Rodriguez and wife Ryvkah Goodman-Rodriguez
expand on Think's contemporary Italian/American concept in this
more upscale, 130-seat space (formerly Caliente). Plans include
a chef's table and an eclectic gourmet menu. A wine-chilling
machine is available to speed the libations along.
(773) 772-7721, think-cafe.com, Sun–Thurs 5–10, Fri–Sat 5–11,
reservations recommended ⚡ ☂

KYOTO SUSHI $$$ / ★★★
2534 N. Lincoln (Wrightwood), Lincoln Park
Japanese
After over 15 years, the original owner sold Kyoto Sushi. But the
liquor license wasn't transferred, and a BYOB was born. Twin
brothers/co-owners Carlo and Melvin Vizconde, who have a
combined experience of over 30 years in places like Kamehachi,
are stationed at the sushi bar. Try one of their "Kyoto Specials,"
like the spicy tuna tataki maki with seared spicy tuna, or the
creamy maki roll wrapped in avocado. A private tatami room for
10–12 people is available on a first-come, first-served basis.
(773) 477-2788, twinsushi.com, Mon closed, Tues–Thurs 5–11, Fri
5–12, Sat–Sun 11–10 ⚡ ♀ Ⓟ

LA AMISTAD $$ / ★
1914 W. Montrose (Wolcott), Ravenswood
American/Mexican
On a block of Montrose where BYOBs are practically the rule, this
casual diner offers a menu equally divided between American and
Mexican chow from the open grill. The owner plans on expanding the dinner menu beyond grilled skirt steaks and fajitas in the
near future. In the meantime, enjoy a quick bite with your own
beer or wine.
(773) 878-5800, Mon–Sat 9–10:30, Sun 9–8 🐟

LA CAZUELA MARISCOS $$ / ★★
6922 N. Clark (Morse), Rogers Park
Mexican
Oysters, shrimp, fried catfish, salmon, red snapper—if Mexican-
style seafood is your thing, this casual, sunny spot is your place. In
fact, the tilapia and shrimp tacos are one of the best deals in town
(don't forget to ask for their hot sauce on the side). La Cazuela
Mariscos carries nonalcoholic margarita and piña colada mixes, so
bring your own tequila or rum to whip up some delish cocktails.
(773) 338-5425, Mon–Thurs 10–10, Fri–Sat 10–11, Sun 9–11
🐝 ⚑ Ⓟ

LA CEBOLLITA GRILL $ / ★★
1807 S. Ashland (18th), Pilsen
Mexican
The no-frills storefront location is deceiving; once inside, you'll
find a roomy, cheery, 50-seat eatery. The Cuedra brothers moved
La Cebollita ("green onion" in Spanish) to this address in 2007,
serving mostly Central Mexican dishes like tamales steamed
in corn husks (only a buck each) and *pozole* (pork stew with
hominy, offered only on weekends). For dinner, there are plenty
of chicken, steak, and seafood entrées, like chicken with mole
poblano sauce and enchiladas.
(312) 492-8447, Mon–Sat 8–10, Sun 9–7 🐝

LA COCINA DE GALARZA RESTAURANT $$ / ★★
2420 W. Fullerton (Western), Logan Square
Puerto Rican
This family-run restaurant has been serving traditional, homemade Puerto Rican food to the neighborhood since 1990. An
enclosed back patio is a well-kept secret and accommodates
private parties up to 50. Virgin piña colada mixes (regular and
strawberry) are available, providing the perfect excuse to break
out the rum.
(773) 235-7377, Mon–Thurs 12–9, Fri–Sat 12–10, Sun
12–8:30 🐝 ⚑

LA FONDA DEL GUSTO $$ / ★★★
1408 N. Milwaukee (Wolcott), Wicker Park
Mexican

An ambitious first-time restaurant for owners Lisa Lee and husband Jose Palomino, this 100-seat, newly remodeled, moderately priced Mexican BYOB is a welcome addition to the area. The menu is a selective sampling of Mexican staples, plus some not-to-be-missed homemade dips and salsas (creamy cilantro-lime, roasted poblano, orange cilantro, ancho chile, roasted mango), which can be ordered on the side to spice up your meal. They offer nonalcoholic mojito, piña colada, and margarita mixes. Limit one bottle of wine or six-pack of beer per couple.
(773) 278-6100, lafondadelgusto.com, Sun–Wed 3:30–10, Thurs–Sat 3:30–11 ⊛ ♀

LA PALAPA $$ / ★★
2000 W. 34th (Damen), McKinley Park
Mexican

Owners Alejandro and Diana Guerra aim for a Mexican beachside experience at this seafood joint. Expect ceviche, shrimp several ways, red snapper, and langostino plates. Locals milk the BYOB policy for all it's worth in the summer, toting bottles of Petron and coolers of Modelo to La Palapa's outdoor patio, an oasis of thatch-covered umbrellas with mariachi bands providing the soundtrack.
(773) 376-9620, lapalapamariscos.com, Sun–Thurs 10–10, Fri–Sat 10–11 ⊛ ✈

LA SIERRA $$ / ★★★
1637 W. Montrose (Ashland), Ravenswood
Nuevo Latino/Brunch

This family restaurant used to serve Ecuadorian and Mexican cuisine, but switched to a Latin-inspired contemporary menu to cater to the changing neighborhood. Gone are the budget tacos, in their place are creations by chef Miguel Quintero and a Cordon Bleu pastry chef. They provide wine glasses, beer mugs, and margarita glasses (even rim salt) upon request.
(773) 549-5538, Sun–Thurs 5–10, Fri–Sat 5–11, Sun brunch 10–3 ⊛

LALIBELA $$ / ★★
5631 N. Ashland (Olive), Edgewater
Ethiopian
Hirut and Samson Ayele poured a lot of love into every detail of
this new Ethiopian eatery, from the imported African furniture
to the made-to-order cuisine. Dishes such as *doro wot* (chicken
with lemon, red pepper, onions, garlic, ginger, cardamom, and
nutmeg—mouth watering yet?) can be ordered anywhere from
"small spice" to "very spicy."
(773) 944-0585, lalibelaonline.com, Mon closed, Tues–Sun
12–10 ⊛

LAN'S $$ / ★★
1507 N. Sedgwick (Blackhawk), Old Town
Chinese
Jimmy Ma, the owner of the original Lan's in Lincoln Park from
1980–1998, is back in Old Town with his original Szechuan and
Mandarin recipes. Old and new customers are welcoming Ma at
his new space (formerly Heat and BBop Lounge); some of Lan's
original staff even work here. Ma prides himself on the homemade pot stickers, Lan's sizzling rice soup, and moo shu pork.
After owning nearly 25 restaurants in the past 31 years, Ma seems
content to stay in one place—for a while, anyway.
(312) 255-9888, lansoldtown.com, 5–12 daily ☂

LATE NIGHT THAI $ / -
1650 W. Belmont (Paulina), Lakeview
Thai
When the owner of Asian Avenue (another BYOB a few doors
down) saw that people kept coming back to this address looking
for the former River Kwai, which served Thai until the wee hours,
he seized the opportunity and opened this appropriately named
eatery. The menu is a streamlined version of Asian Avenue's, and
the concept is fast, cheap food and no-frills atmosphere (think
late night + drunk people = no glassware).
(773) 327-9946, latenightthai.com, Mon closed, Tues–Sun 9–5a
⊛ ⑤ ⒜ₜₘ

LE CONAKRY $ / ★★
2049 W. Howard (Hoyne), Rogers Park
African
The menu is primarily focused on French West African cuisine
(Guinea, Senegal, Mali, Ivory Coast), with a Nigerian chef adding
his own influences. The food is slow-cooked and made-to-order,
so don't expect fast food (or service). But the savory dishes are
worth it, especially the yassa fish or chicken and peanut butter
soup (earn brownie points with the staff if you can order your
meal in French). The main dining area seats 35, and a private
party room accommodates another 100.
(773) 262-6955, 11–10 daily 🐶 🍷

LE GEE $ / ★★
1810 W. Montrose (Wolcott), Ravenswood
Pan-Asian
In Wing Lee's former space, Le Gee caters mostly to takeout
customers emptying out from the Brown Line. But this casual
BYOB also has a small dining room for its surprisingly extensive
menu of Thai and Chinese seafood and wok noodle dishes. There
are a few wine glasses available, and staff will chill your bottles in
the fridge on request.
(773) 334-6589, Mon–Fri 11–9:30, Sat–Sun 4–9:30 🐶

LEMONGRASS $ / ★★★
1520 W. Taylor (Laflin), University Village/Little Italy
Thai
You could throw a rock and hit a few Thai restaurants on this
section of Taylor Street. But Lemongrass (same owners and menu
as Sweet Tamarind, another BYOB) offers a more unique and
extensive menu than others—nearly 100 items—most with a
Northern Thai influence. Appetizers are a highlight, especially
the lemongrass rolls, steamed mussels, and Thai sausage (made
with ginger, cilantro, and peanuts). Entrées include lemongrass
noodles and khao soy, a curry soup with egg noodles, lime, shal-
lots, hot peppers, and meat. Sticky rice with mango and coconut
cream, lemon tarts, or pumpkin custard help finish things off on
a sweet note.
(312) 829-0800, lemongrass1520thai.com, Mon–Sat 11–10, Sun
closed 🐶

LE'S PHO $ / ★
4925 N. Broadway (Argyle), Uptown
Vietnamese
Tucked away in a shopping plaza in an area where it's apparently
difficult to get a liquor license, this 50-seat, family-oriented
noodle shop has been in business since 1994. Le's serves nearly
50 different types of *pho*, or huge steaming bowls (aren't they
really pools?) of beef broth. Do like the locals do and order a day's
worth of meals to go during Le's morning hours.
(773) 784-8723, Mon–Thurs 8–9, Fri 8–9:30, Sat 7:30–9:30, Sun
7:30–9 ⊛ Ⓟ

LINCOLN PARK'S NOODLE HOUSE $$ / ★★
2428 N. Ashland (Fullerton), Lincoln Park
Japanese/Thai
The BYOB policy here attracts budget-conscious diners seeking
a bite to eat before hitting the local bars. The space features
exposed timber and brick walls, plush pillows at each seat, and a
private party room that accommodates up to 35. The menu cov-
ers typical Thai terrain, from noodle soups to curries to entrées,
and the sushi bar offers maki and sushi by the platter or à la carte.
Parties of 10 or more may need to BYO stemware, so call ahead.
(773) 248-6680, lincolnparknoodlehouse.com, Mon closed,
Tues–Thurs 11–10:30, Fri–Sat 11–11, Sun 4:30–10:30 ⊛ ♈

LITTLE BROTHER'S $ / ★
818 W. Fullerton (Halsted), Lincoln Park
Korean
This may be one of the narrowest eateries in the city, but owners
have made judicious use of the space and created a cute spot
for noshing on Korean rice bowls. The food here is admittedly
"Americanized Korean" but delicious nonetheless. Expect rice
bowls topped with meat or tofu, veggies, and the obligatory fried
egg, customized with one of three sauces: sweet soy and brown
sugar, cilantro and chili, or spicy chili.
(773) 661-6482, Mon–Fri 11–10 (closed 3:30–4:30), Sat 11–10,
Sun closed ⊛

THE LITTLE INDIA $$ / ★
1109 W. Bryn Mawr (Winthrop), Edgewater
Indian
Owner Mumtal Rizvi (Zam Zam) touts "Indian fusion cuisine"
here, but in this case "fusion" means pan-Indian, or a marriage of
Northern and Southern Indian cooking. So there's equal opportunity for vegetarians and carnivores to enjoy a meal in a cozy,
remodeled place just steps from the Bryn Mawr stop on the Red
Line. Highlights are the chicken madras (chicken cooked in curry
and coconut milk), tikka masala, and, for those who really like it
hot, lamb vindaloo.
(773) 728-7012, littleindiaonline.com, Sun–Thurs 11–10, Fri–Sat
11–10:30, reservations recommended on weekends ⊗

L'OLIVO $$ / ★★
1602 E. Algonquin Rd. (Meacham), Schaumburg
Italian
There aren't many places to BYOB in this area, but due to a clause
in L'Olivo's lease, they're restricted from obtaining a liquor license.
Gourmet thin-crust pizzas are their specialty, especially the BBQ
chicken with smoked gouda and mozz, chicken and roasted
potato with rosemary and garlic, and the mushroom lover's variety, a blend of spinach, cheese, and three types of 'shrooms. The
100-seat space, located in the Park Place shopping plaza, is closed
to the public on Sundays but available for private parties (perfect
for easy-on-the-wallet bridal showers or family get-togethers).
(847) 397-9900, lolivo.net, Mon–Thurs 10:30–8:30, Fri–Sat
11:30–10, Sun closed ⊗ Ⓟ

LOS CAMINOS DE MICHOACAN $$ / -
3948 N. Sheridan (Irving Park), Lakeview
Mexican
At this diner-style joint, Latin music pumps out of the jukebox
and Univision plays on overhead TVs while families and late-
night crowds enjoy a full range of homemade, authentic Mexican
food. Located steps from the Red Line's Sheridan stop, this place
serves full dinners, from carne asada to fajitas to several seafood
options (red snapper, shrimp) and pork chops sautéed in green or
red sauce. Or choose from the usual à la carte options, like tacos,
burritos, sopes, and tortas.
(773) 296-9709, Mon–Thurs 10–3a, Fri–Sat 10–5a, Sun
10–3a ⊗

LOS NOPALES $$ / ★★
4544 N. Western (Wilson), Lincoln Square
Mexican/Brunch

This family-run Lincoln Square spot has proved to be one of
the brightest BYOB stars in the city. Serving updated versions of
regional Mexican food, Los Nopales' highlights are homemade
moles, creamy flan (flavors change daily), braised meats, and the
namesake salad, a concoction of chilled cactus, jicama, avocado,
tomato, and mango chipotle dressing. A private party room in the
back accommodates up to 50.
(773) 334-3149, losnopalesrestaurant.com, Mon closed, Tues–Sun
10–10, reservations recommended on weekends ⚲ ♍

LUC THANG $ / ★★
1524 N. Ashland (Pierce), Wicker Park
Pan-Asian

Locals swear by this no-frills spot, which serves solid Thai,
Vietnamese, and Chinese fare. Those who prefer traditional
pad Thai will appreciate Luc Thang's version, doused in a spicy
tomato-based sauce. Authentic ingredients are used throughout
the entire menu, like the panang, which is prepared with curry
powder instead of the usual paste for a more subtle flavor. A few
cheap wine glasses and corkscrews are available on request.
(773) 395-3907, Mon–Thurs 11–10, Fri–Sat 11–11, Sun 3–10 ♻

LUCIA'S RISTORANTE $$$ / ★★★
1825 W. North (Honore), Wicker Park
Italian

Regulars who frequented the original Barcello's on Milwaukee
(now Mado) will be ecstatic to find the same owners behind this
fine-dining BYOB. The kitchen crafts freshly made pastas, steaks,
veal, chops, seafood, and heavenly desserts. One bite into the
pumpkin ravioli with sage butter, prosciutto, and walnuts or the
homemade spinach potato dumplings in bleu cheese and mascar-
pone and you'll be singing Lucia's praises all the way home. Full
beverage service provided on request.
(773) 292-9700, Mon–Thurs 5–10, Fri–Sat 5–11, Sun closed,
reservations recommended on weekends ♻ 🎋

LUZZAT RESTAURANT $ / ★★
1505 W. Jarvis (Greenview), Rogers Park
Indian
This casual 30-seat eatery, located in Jarvis Square, a charming area with independently owned cafés, shops, wine stores, and restaurants, offers authentic Indian cuisine away from the hustle of Devon Avenue. Daily specials are available along with a full menu of classic Indian dishes, like samosa (fried turnovers filled with vegetables or meat), tandoori (chicken baked in a clay oven), and *matar paneer*, a dish made with an Indian soft cheese and peas in a spicy sauce.
(773) 764-1065, Wed–Mon 12–9, Tues closed ⊛

M. HENRY $ / ★★★
5707 N. Clark (Hollywood), Edgewater
Contemporary American/Brunch
Homemade breads and pastries tempt from the bakery counter as you enter this comfy neighborhood lunch and brunch destination. Just as tempting is the dine-in menu, which includes savory dishes (lemon crab and shrimp cake benedict) as well as sweet (vanilla and egg custard brioche bread pudding topped with warm peaches and blackberries). They'll provide Champagne glasses and buckets on request.
(773) 561-1600, mhenry.net, Mon closed, Tues–Fri 7–2:30, Sat–Sun 8–3 ⊛ ⌁

MACHU PICCHU $$ / ★★★
3856 N. Ashland (Byron), Lakeview
Peruvian
New owners took over this Peruvian steakhouse in 2009 and, in the interest of attracting budget-conscious diners, are holding off on applying for a liquor license during the economic downturn. The menu includes grilled sirloins, several seafood dishes, chicken, ceviche, and entrée-portioned soups. Champagne flutes, wine glasses, ice buckets, and corkscrews are available on request.
(773) 472-0471, Mon–Thurs 12–10, Fri–Sat 12–11, Sun 12–9 ⊛

MADO $$$ / ★★★
1647 N. Milwaukee (Concord), Wicker Park
Eclectic

Mado's cuisine is often categorized as Italian, and while there
are obvious Mediterranean influences throughout the dishes
(especially in the antipasti, vegetables, and charcuterie), seasonal
ingredients sourced from local producers strongly dictate what
you'll see on the rotating menu. Entrées range from fresh rainbow
trout to spit-roasted pork belly to grilled sweetbreads. Forget
classification and just focus on the simple, superbly seasoned
food. (Pork lovers, this is your place.)
(773) 342-2340, madorestaurantchicago.com, Mon closed,
Tues–Thurs 5–10, Fri–Sat 5–11, Sun 5–9, reservations
recommended ⊛

MAMACITA'S $$ / ★★
2439 N. Clark (Fullerton), Lincoln Park
Mexican

In a café-like setting with Mexican accents, Mamacita's puts an
updated spin on traditional Mexican cuisine. Try tilapia Santa
Cruz, mushroom and poblano pizza, duck breast quesadillas, or
portabella mushroom enchiladas with mole sauce. There's nonalcoholic sangria mix for your bottle of Spanish red and several
tropical fruit juices to blend with Champagne or vodka.
(773) 404-7788, mamacitarestaurant.com, Mon–Thurs 10–10,
Fri–Sat 10–1:30a, Sun 9–9 ⊛

MANDARIN KITCHEN $$ / -
2143 S. Archer (Cermak), Chinatown
Chinese

What doesn't this place have? There's dim sum (steamed dumplings), congee (rice porridge), chef's specials (sizzling rice, seafood
dishes), and a few dozen entrées on the family-style menu (pick
any three for $22.95). But wait, that's not it; tons of noodle soups
and "American Favorites" (moo shu pork, cashew chicken) are
also available.
(312) 328-0228, Mon–Thurs 11–10, Fri–Sun 11–11 ⊛

MANEE THAI #2 $ / ★★
1546 W. Chicago (Ashland), Noble Square
Pan-Asian

These are the same folks behind Manee Thai #1, which burned
down in 2008. At this new location, they've made vast improve-
ments to the space (formerly Thai Castle), added a fresh-fruit
smoothie bar, and recreated Manee Thai #1's menu, a mix of
mostly Thai and some Chinese and Japanese cuisine. Plans to
rebuild the original site are in the works.
(312) 733-3339, maneethaionline.com, Mon–Thurs 11–10,
Fri–Sat 11–11, Sun 12–10 ☺

MARK'S CHOP SUEY $ / ★
3343 N. Halsted (Buckingham), Lakeview
Chinese

In business for over 30 years, Mark's Chop Suey is one of those
Chinese takeout joints that didn't know it was BYOB until
regulars started inquiring whether they could bring their own
booze. So the owner upgraded the dining room (small and casual
but cute) and now encourages customers to bring their own wine
or beer. Water glasses and corkscrews are available on request.
(773) 281-9090, Mon closed, Tues–Sun 3–11 ☺

MARRAKECH CUISINE $ / ★★★
1413 N. Ashland (Blackhawk), Noble Square
Moroccan

The retail storefront, which sells imported Moroccan lamps and
other curiosities, leads to a comfortable, casual neighborhood
ethnic eatery. Entrées rarely go over the $10 mark, and each dish
is made-to-order with imported Moroccan spices and ingredients.
Choose from vegetarian appetizers like *taktaouka* (mashed eggplant with tomatoes, cilantro, garlic) and lentil salad (made with
spicy *harissa* sauce) as well as an interesting variety of tagines,
kebabs, and couscous entrées.
(773) 227-6451, marrakechcuisine.com, Mon closed, Tues–Sun
5–11 ↗

MASOULEH $$ / ★★
6653 N. Clark (Wallen), Rogers Park
Middle Eastern
You won't find hummus or baba ghanouj here. But you will find
Persian cuisine "with a Northern twist," which means *shishandaz*
(eggplant with walnut and pomegranate sauce), *cheimeh bademjan*
(a stew of eggplant, peas, and beef), lamb shank with mushroom
sauce, and a variety of kebabs.
(773) 262-2227, Mon closed, Tues–Thurs 5–9, Fri 5–10, Sat
12–10, Sun 12–8 ✆

MATSU YAMA $$$$ / ★★★
1059 W. Belmont (Seminary), Lakeview
Japanese
The atmosphere here is somewhere between an older, more
traditional sushi spot (New Tokyo, Kamehachi) and one of the
new, sleek sushi bars. The ambience is clean and contemporary
but not trendy, and the menu is an extensive list of sushi and
maki (the Godzilla and firecracker maki are highlights), as well
as a growing selection of Japanese fare from the kitchen (small
plates, tempura).
(773) 327-8838, Mon–Thurs 4–11, Fri–Sat 11:30–2:30, 4–12,
Sun 11–2:30, 4–10, reservations recommended on weekends ✆

MAY STREET CAFÉ $$$ / ★★
1146 W. Cermak (May), Pilsen
Nuevo Latino
Neon green isn't my favorite paint color, but it serves as a beacon
of light for May Street Café, which is located in a bleak industrial
area. That same light will lead you to an intimate, comfortable,
gourmet eatery, driven by chef Mario Santiago's inventive, Latin-
inspired, visually expressive cuisine.
(312) 421-4442, maystcafe.com, Mon closed, Tues–Thurs 5–10,
Fri–Sat 5–11, Sun 5–9, reservations recommended ✆ Ⓟ

MEDICI ON 57TH $ / ★★
1327 E. 57th (Kenwood), Hyde Park
American/Brunch
An adjacent bakery provides specialty breads and pastries (asiago cheese baguettes, cinnamon rolls) for this lunch, dinner, and weekend brunch spot, which has been in the area for over 40 years. Medici's popular rooftop terrace and recent Obama sightings are two more reasons to stop by.
(773) 667-7394, medici57.com, Mon–Thurs 11–11, Fri 11–12, Sat 9–12, Sun 9–11 🐝 🏴

MEI SHUNG $$ / ★★
5511 N. Broadway (Catalpa), Edgewater
Chinese/Taiwanese
Where else in town can you order a complete, authentic Taiwanese dinner for eight people for less than 100 bucks? Mei Shung specializes in "family dinners," or multi-course Mandarin/Taiwanese meals served on lazy Susans. Not sure what to order? The orange chicken, Taiwanese sausage, onion cake, and steamed bean curd roll are all favorites here. Ask for the "specials" menu for a list of more authentic Taiwanese options.
(773) 728-5778, meishungtogo.com, Mon closed, Tues–Thurs 11:30–10, Fri 11:30–11, Sat 12–11, Sun 12–9:30 🐝

MISS ASIA $–$$ / ★★
434 W. Diversey (Pine Grove), Lakeview
Pan-Asian
The range of Asian influences on Miss Asia's menu is unparalleled. About half of the dishes are Thai, but then the choices branch out to Cambodian banana blossom salad, Malaysian laksa, Mongolian barbecue, Korean shrimp pancakes, and Indonesian curry, with a few stabs at Japanese, Indian, Vietnamese, Chinese, and Filipino cuisine. New owners have completely updated the dining room (formerly Thai Me Up). Only beer and wine are allowed.
(773) 248-3999, missasiacuisine.com, Sun–Thurs 11–10, Fri–Sat 11–11 🐝

MISTA $ / ★
2931 N. Broadway (Oakdale), Lakeview
Italian
Thin, "cracker crust" pizza is the specialty at this cute, café-like
spot. The kitchen uses nearly 100% organic ingredients for
its made-to-order pizzas, salads, dressings, wraps, lasagnas
(noodles made on-site), and daily specials, which are posted on a
chalkboard by the register. They may have a corkscrew or some
plastic cups available for your beer or wine; otherwise, you're on
your own.
(773) 698-6688, mistapizza.com, Mon closed, Tues–Sat 11–10,
Sun 12–9 ⊛ ⋗

MISTA $ / ★
5351 N. Clark (Balmoral), Andersonville
Italian
This sister location (there are plans for a third locale in the Loop)
offers the same organic menu and a slightly larger space, so it's
even more conducive to BYOB dining.
(773) 506-1500, mistapizza.com, Mon–Sat 11–10, Sun 12–9
⊛ ⋗

MIXTECO GRILL $$$ / ★★★
1601 W. Montrose (Ashland), Ravenswood
Nuevo Latino/Brunch
Chef/co-owner Raul Arreola (Fonda del Mar) and partners serve
regional Mexican cuisine to a packed house nightly. Standouts
include the wood-grilled calamari and arugula salad, sopes,
wood-grilled mahi-mahi with peanut mole sauce, pork chops
with mole sauce, and mashed sweet potatoes.
(773) 868-1601, Mon closed, Tues–Thurs 5–10, Fri–Sat 5–11, Sun
10:30–2:30 (brunch), 5–9 (dinner), reservations recommended ⊛

MYSORE WOODLANDS $ / ★★
2548 W. Devon (Rockwell), West Rogers Park
Indian/Vegetarian

With so many choices for Indian food in this area, it's often
difficult to decide where to go. If a vegetarian-only menu, BYOB
policy, updated decor, and focus on dine-in service (instead of delivery or carryout) are on your wish list, then Mysore Woodlands
is your place. But once inside, you're hit with multiple choices
once again: Will it be the *masala dosai* (thin crepes with spicy
chutney), *vada* (lentil donuts), *channa batura* (tandoor-grilled
bread with chickpeas), or one of their curries? Better order several
just to be on the safe side.
(773) 338-8160, Sun–Thurs 11:30–9:30, Fri–Sat 11–10 ⊛ Ⓟ

MYTHOS $$$ / ★★
2030 W. Montrose (Seeley), Ravenswood
Greek

Co-owner/chef Vicky Zervas plays homage to her grandparents
and great-grandparents at this storefront BYOB with their
Northern Greek recipes, like the *pastichio* (baked casserole with
béchamel sauce) and homemade spreads like *tzatziki*, *tara-
mosalata*, and *skordalia* (made with potatoes, garlic, olive oil, and
capers). The food is slow-cooked and service is a little spotty, so
relax, open a bottle of chilled white, and nosh on appetizers while
you wait for your entrée.
(773) 334-2000, mythoschicago.com, Mon closed, Tues–Sun
5–10 ⤡ ⚑

NAN'S SUSHI & CHINESE $–$$$ / ★★★
2360 N. Lincoln (Fullerton), Lincoln Park
Chinese/Japanese

The name says it all. Expect an extensive Chinese *and* sushi menu
at this charming neighborhood eatery. Sake cups, wine and beer
glasses, ice buckets, and corkscrews are available on request. After
5:00, parking is available at Children's Memorial Hospital across
the street; owners will pay for half. Such a deal.
(773) 935-5900, nanssushi.com, Sun–Thurs 11–10, Fri–Sat
11–11 ⤡

NEW JEANNY'S RESTAURANT $ / ★★
1053 W. Belmont (Seminary), Lakeview
Chinese

When new owners took over from the original Jeanny's in 2005, they opted out of a liquor license since most of their business is takeout and delivery. But there's a spacious dining room to enjoy one of the 20 dinner specials offered nightly from 5–10, most under $10. Choose from sweet and sour chicken, Szechuan vegetable, Mongolian beef, Szechuan shrimp, and others; they all come with steamed rice, an egg roll, and soup. An unusual assortment of stemware is available (no doubt left from the days when there was a full bar).
(773) 248-1133, newjeannys.com, Mon 11:30–10, Tues closed, Wed–Thurs 11:30–10, Fri–Sat 11:30–10:30, Sun 12–10 ⊛

NEW SAIGON $ / ★
5000 N. Broadway (Argyle), Uptown
Vietnamese

You have to love a place with the simple slogan, "We cook what you want." If you're looking for truly authentic Vietnamese cooking in this neighborhood, you won't get any more genuine than this place. A husband-wife team has served as manager and cook (respectively) at New Saigon since 1991. And the menu? As old school as their cash-only policy.
(773) 334-3322, 10–10 daily ⊛ 🖾

NEW TOKYO $$$$ / ★
3139 N. Broadway (Briar), Lakeview
Japanese

If you're looking for a hip, trendy sushi bar, skip New Tokyo. But if traditional Japanese cuisine and fresh, high-quality sushi is your thing, New Tokyo can't be beat. For nearly 15 years, this tiny neighborhood place (owners also run Sushi Luxe in Andersonville) has offered a wide variety of Japanese apps, soups, entrées, and bentos. The real stars, however, are the excellent sushi and maki choices, made with fish that is flown in daily (you can't say that about most Chicago sushi places). Specials rotate seasonally.
(773) 248-1193, 12–11 daily ⊛ 🏴

NILE RESTAURANT $$ / ★
1611 E. 55th (Cornell), Hyde Park
Middle Eastern
A reliable neighborhood spot for Middle Eastern cuisine. Highlights include the kebabs, especially the filet mignon and lamb
varieties. The glasses they provide to BYOB customers are also
used to serve tea and coffee, so you may want to bring your own
stemware. No hard alcohol allowed.
(773) 324-9499, Mon–Sat 11–9, Sun 12–8 ⊛

90 MILES CUBAN CAFÉ $ / -
3101 N. Clybourn (Barry), Lakeview
Cuban
This Cuban café, named after the distance between Cuba and
the United States, created a major buzz when it opened in 2008.
Husband-wife team Alberto and Christina Gonzalez are behind
this venture, which offers breakfast, lunch, and an à la carte
dinner menu. Entrées such as *lechon* (roasted pork) and *ropa viejo*
(shredded beef) go for around $10 while sides like fried plantains
and empanadas fetch another $2–$3.
(773) 248-2822, 90milescubancafe.com, Mon–Sat 8–8, Sun
9–6 ⊛ ☂

90 MILES CUBAN CAFÉ $ / -
2540 W. Armitage (Stave), Logan Square
Cuban
This second, larger location (formerly Calvin's BBQ) seats about
40, with space for another 40 on the outdoor patio, and offers a
few more menu items than its Clybourn sibling, like the tilapia
sandwich and whole red snapper with *tostones*. Plastic cups and
ice are available; otherwise there's no beverage service.
(773) 227-2822, 90milescubancafe.com, Mon–Sat 8–8, Sun
9–6 ⊛ ☂

THE NOODLE $ / -
2336 S. Wentworth (23rd), Chinatown
Vietnamese
Located on the southern end of the strip of Wentworth that runs
through the heart of Chinatown, The Noodle is a casual spot for
pho (beef noodle soup), rice plates, and vermicelli noodle bowls.
BYOB is not common here (they specialize in smoothies and
coffee drinks), but it is allowed.
(312) 674-1168, Sun–Thurs 10–10, Fri–Sat 10–11 ⊛

NOODLE ZONE $–$$ / ★
5427 N. Clark (Rascher), Andersonville
Pan-Asian
This place serves traditional and contemporary Pan-Asian dishes
(Japanese, sushi, Vietnamese, Thai, Chinese) in an updated but
comfortable atmosphere. Menu items such as the flavorful green
curry with chicken can be ordered mild, medium, or spicy. Beverage service is pretty erratic.
(773) 293-1089, noodlezonechicago.net, Mon–Thurs 11:30–
9:30, Fri–Sat 11:30–10, Sun 12–9:30 ⊛

NOODLES ETC. $ / ★
1333 E. 57th (Kenwood), Hyde Park
Pan-Asian
An open kitchen and quick service give this noodle shop a fast-
paced, hectic atmosphere. The menu is heavy on Thai stir-fry, the
house specialty, but for variety's sake there are several Japanese,
Chinese, and Vietnamese options.
(773) 947-8787, noodlesetc.com, Mon–Sat 11–10, Sun 11:30–
9:30 ⊛

NOODLES IN THE POT $ / ★★
2453 N. Halsted (Altgeld), Lincoln Park
Thai
If you enjoy Joy's Noodles & Rice (a Lakeview BYOB), you'll love
this place, where the same owners offer an identical menu. But
the space couldn't be more different; instead of the large, airy
room at Joy's, Noodles in the Pot's dining room is spread out over
three, narrow, disjointed spaces. But the outdoor garden patio is a
relaxing place to grab a bite in warmer months.
(773) 975-6177, noodlesinthepot.com, Sun–Thurs 11–10, Fri–Sat
11–11 ⊛ ⚑

NOODLES PARTY $ / ★★
4205 W. Lawrence (Keeler), Northwest Side
Pan-Asian
Besides winning one of this book's best restaurant name awards, this cozy spot serves everything from Filipino (*lumpia*) to Thai (chicken satay) to Chinese (wonton soup) and Japanese (udon noodle soup, sushi). Owner Kiti Pong's brother runs Zen Noodle in Wicker Park, which could explain the inspiration for the Pan-Asian stir-fry recipes.
(773) 205-0505, noodlesparty.com, Mon–Fri 11–9:30, Sat–Sun 12–9:30 🐝

NOOKIES $$ / ★★
1746 N. Wells (Eugenie), Old Town
American/Brunch
In 1973, Michael Mitsoglou created Nookies with an elevated café concept in mind. Locals responded to the fresh and tasty breakfast menu, generous portions, exceptional coffee, and comfortable atmosphere. Three locations later, Nookies is now synonymous with breakfast in Chicago. This location—the original—also serves lunch and dinner (see Web site for menu).
(312) 337-2454, nookiesrestaurants.net, Mon–Sat 6:30–10, Sun 6:30–9 🐝 🕊

NOOKIES TOO $ / ★★
2114 N. Halsted (Willow), Lincoln Park
American/Brunch
Nookies may have counter service and the occasional server with a pencil tucked behind her ear, but this is definitely not "diner" food. Only the freshest of ingredients are used for their breakfast sandwiches (smoked gouda, veggies, eggs), the hangover helper skillet (hash browns, chili, poached eggs), and other modern takes on breakfast fare. Freshly squeezed OJ and other juices are available to mix with your Champagne or vodka.
(773) 327-1400, nookiesrestaurants.net, Mon–Thurs 7–3:30, Fri–Sat 24 hours, Sun 7–5 🐝

NOOKIES TREE $$ / ★★★
3334 N. Halsted (Buckingham), Lakeview
American/Brunch

This location offers the most extensive dinner menu (New York strip streak, Honshu salmon, penne with chicken sausage) of all three Nookies, and the 'hood packs this place for weekend brunch—especially on the outdoor patio—making this a popular spot to BYOB. Several great wine stores are nearby if you're empty-handed. Champagne flutes, stemware, ice buckets, and corkscrews are available on request.

(773) 248-9888, nookiesrestaurants.net, Sun–Thurs 7–midnight, Fri–Sat 24 hours ⊛ 🏴

NUEVO LÉON RESTAURANT $$ / ★★
1515 W. 18th (Laflin), Pilsen
Mexican

The Gutierrez family established this lively 180-seat restaurant in 1962, and it has been an anchor in the Pilsen neighborhood ever since. Now run by the third generation, Nuevo Léon pays tribute to the family's Northern Mexican roots with dishes such as homemade *queso con chorizo*, carne asada, and *especial cazuela* (rib eye with poblano peppers and panela cheese), served by staff in traditional Mexican garb. They'll provide garnishes for your margaritas (rim salt, lime) on request.

(312) 421-1517, nuevoleonrestaurant.com, 7–midnight daily
⊛ 💵 ATM

OH FUSION $$$ / ★★★
3911 N. Sheridan (Dakin), Lakeview
Japanese/Thai

The owner changed the name (formerly Katachi), added Thai to the menu, and remodeled with a clean, contemporary, black-and-white decor. Katachi's sushi menu remains (including the popular ocean drive maki rolls), but new items added include Japanese appetizers (gyoza, tempura) and Thai noodle and rice dishes. They're open late on weeknights.

(773) 880-5340, Sun–Thurs 11–2a, Fri–Sat 11–11 ⊛ 🏴

OLD JERUSALEM $$ / ★★
1411 N. Wells (Schiller), Old Town
Middle Eastern
This neighborhood place has been serving high-quality, delicious, made-to-order Lebanese food since 1976. It's a great place to grab a bite before heading to Second City, Zanies, or any of the watering holes in the area (or just strolling down historic Wells Street). The mouthwatering *shawerma* sandwiches include thick slices of lamb or filet mignon piled into a pita with onions, tomatoes, lettuce, and freshly made tahini sauce.
(312) 944-0459, oldjerusalemrestaurant.com, 11–11 daily ⚞ ⚟

OLIVE MOUNTAIN $$ / ★
610 Davis (Chicago), Evanston
Middle Eastern
One of the oldest restaurants in the downtown Evanston area, Olive Mountain offers an extensive menu of Mediterranean (and a few American) appetizers, salads, and entrées. Fresh seafood tops the daily specials menu. They provide water glasses, ice, and corkscrews on request.
(847) 475-0380, olivemountainrestaurant.com, Mon–Thurs 11–9:30, Fri 11–10:30, Sat 12–10:30, Sun 12–9 ✪

OODLES OF NOODLES $ / ★★
2540 N. Clark (Deming), Lincoln Park
Pan-Asian
About half of the menu is devoted to various Asian noodle dishes, from Mongolian noodle soup to stir-fried udon to pad Thai and drunken noodles. The rest is a hodgepodge of Asian appetizers, fried and steamed rice dishes, and maki rolls. Dim sum is available on the weekends. They'll keep special beer glasses on hand for regular customers. (Be sure to check out the oodles of books displayed above the hostess stand.)
(773) 975-1090, onoodles.com, Mon–Thurs 11–10, Fri–Sat 11–10:30, Sun 11:30–10 ✪

OPART THAI HOUSE $ / ★★
4658 N. Western (Eastwood), Lincoln Square
Thai
This long-standing Thai eatery is located on what could be called
"Thai restaurant row." The competition doesn't seem to be a
problem for this place, which remodeled a few years ago with
new hardwood floors, skylights, additional seating, and beautiful
Thai woodwork and traditional art. Opart specializes in beef
dishes, like the tiger cry, Opart beef, or *neau sa-ded*, charbroiled
beef served with hot sauce.
(773) 989-8517, opartthai.com, Sun–Thurs 11–10, Fri–Sat
11–11 ⊛

ORANGE $ / ★
3231 N. Clark (Belmont), Lakeview
Contemporary American/Brunch
This location dropped their dinner menu but still offers their
specialty: an eclectic brunch menu of creative pancake, French
toast, and egg dishes. Their juice bar is a mixologist's playground,
with a dozen or so freshly squeezed fruit and vegetable juices
available. Try the tomato/celery combo for a wicked Bloody Mary
mix, or blend their fruit juices with your own bottle of brut
Champagne or sparkling wine for a customized mimosa. Mix and
match, create new cocktails—the sky's the limit.
(773) 549-4400, orangerestaurantchicago.com, Mon–Fri 9–3:30,
Sat–Sun 8–3:30 ⊛ ⚑

ORANGE $ / ★
730 W. Grand (Halsted), River West
Contemporary American/Brunch
Finally—a BYOB with valet parking. This one's open late on
Thursdays thru Saturdays (think Denny's for foodies), but
unfortunately they do not allow BYOB or serve from their juice
bar after 10 p.m. Expect Orange's standard menu at this corner
bi-level spot, which is next to Funky Buddha Lounge.
(312) 942-0300, orangerestaurantchicago.com, Sun–Wed 8–3,
Thurs–Sat 8–4a ⊛ ⚑

OVER EASY CAFÉ $ / ★★
4943 N. Damen (Ainslie), Ravenswood
Eclectic/Brunch
Inventive breakfast and lunch dishes such as banana-spiked French toast, tofu *chilaquiles*, and green chili chicken *tortas* take center stage at this popular neighborhood spot, where BYOB is allowed but not too common. A few diners do bring their own Champagne, however, which mixes beautifully with Over Easy's freckled or black-eyed OJs (orange juice mixed with strawberry or blackberry purees).
(773) 506-2605, overeasycafechicago.com, Mon closed, Tues–Sat 7–3, Sun 8–3 🐝

PANANG $ / ★★
800 N. Clark (Chicago), Near North
Thai
Panang is a casual place to relax and refuel after a hard day of shopping on the Mag Mile. The typical Thai dishes are here (crab Rangoon, pad Thai, *lard nar*), but a few choices, like sunshine beef, shrimp cake, and Phuket noodles, cater to more adventurous eaters.
(312) 573-9999, panangthai.com, Sun–Thurs 11–9:30, Fri–Sat 11–10:30 🐝

PAPACITO'S MEXICAN GRILLE $ / -
2960 N. Lincoln (Wellington), Lakeview
Mexican
This diner-style spot offers several surprises, like the goat cheese nachos and fish tacos, a tasty affair of marinated and grilled tilapia topped with *pico de gallo* and pineapple sauce. The Mexican-with-a-twist theme extends to the dinner options, like the Mexican pizza (topped with avocado puree, beans, peppers, tomatoes, onions, and cheese), shrimp in spicy *diablo* sauce, and grilled chicken with mole. No hard alcohol allowed, and you're on your own for beverage service.
(773) 327-5240, papacitosrestaurant.com, Sun–Thurs 9–9, Fri–Sat 9–10 🐝 🏴

PENNY'S NOODLE SHOP $ / ★
3400 N. Sheffield (Roscoe), Lakeview
Thai

There are several Penny's throughout Chicagoland, but this is
the only city location that's BYOB (due to the fact that they only
have one bathroom). Offering a Westernized approach to Thai
cuisine, the food here is reliably fresh, tasty, and quick, and the
service is always fast and friendly. Try the gyoza or tom yum soup
for starters, then move on to the reliable pad Thai, wonton soup
(BBQ pork, shrimp and pork dumplings in broth), Thai ravioli, or
sesame beef.

(773) 281-8222, pennysnoodleshop.com, Mon closed, Tues–Thurs
11–10, Fri–Sat 11–10:30, Sun 11–10 ⊕ ⚑

PENNY'S NOODLE SHOP $ / ★★
320 S. Happ Rd. (Mt. Pleasant), Northfield
Thai

One of the newest Penny's locations, you'll find the same, reliable
menu of updated versions of pad Thai, chicken satay, and noodle
soups here. The owner is considering applying for a liquor
license, so call ahead to make sure they're still BYOB.

(847) 446-4747, pennysnoodleshop.com, Mon–Fri 11–9, Sat–Sun
4–10 ⊕

PHO 888 $$ / ★★
1137 W. Argyle (Broadway), Uptown
Vietnamese

If you have not discovered this hole-in-the-wall Vietnamese place,
you are missing one of the city's true culinary treasures. Though
it's in a tiny, cramped storefront (like most places on this block),
Pho 888 offers classic examples of dozens of Vietnamese dishes,
like the shrimp spring rolls and grilled pork sandwich served on a
French baguette (baked at nearby bakery Ban Le), not to mention
their namesake dish, which offers a week's worth of broth.

(773) 907-8838, Mon 9–2, Tues–Thurs 9–9, Fri–Sun 9–10 ⊕

PHO 777 $ / ★★
1063–65 W. Argyle (Winthrop), Uptown
Vietnamese

Noodle shops dominate Argyle Street between Broadway and
Sheridan, dubbed "Little Saigon," where BYOBs are now pretty
much the standard. Families convene at this noodle shop for the
ubiquitous *pho* or a dinner of crispy-skin baked fish or marinated
beef. There's a $15 minimum for credit cards.
(773) 561-9909, Mon 9:30–10, Tues closed, Wed–Thurs 9:30–10,
Fri–Sun 9–10 ✈

PHO VIET $$ / ★★
4941 N. Broadway (Argyle), Uptown
Vietnamese

New owners took over this space (formerly Ba Mien Viet Food
Court), removed the Vietnamese knickknacks, and updated
the decor. The dance floor is still here, however. That and the
occasionally unleashed karaoke machine make Pho Viet the
perfect setup for large parties. The mammoth menu offers over
150 choices for *pho*, hot pots, lemongrass entrées, and other
traditional Vietnamese specialties.
(773) 769-1284, Wed–Mon 9–10, Tues closed ✈

PHO XE LUA $ / -
1021 W. Argyle (Kenmore), Uptown
Vietnamese

This small, unpretentious noodle shop caters to the local
Vietnamese population and business community. The 200-item
menu does carry a wide range of familiar fare (*pho*, spring rolls,
Vietnamese noodle and rice dishes) but has a bit more variety
than typical spots on this block. Check your expectations for
ambience and service at the door, and bring your own corkscrew
and bottle opener.
(773) 275-7512, Fri–Wed 9–9, Thurs closed ✈

PHO XUA $ / ★
1020 W. Argyle (Kenmore), Uptown
Chinese/Vietnamese
Like so many restaurants in this area, Pho Xua's menu really packs
it in, with nearly 200 items to choose from. Sprinkled among the
Vietnamese standards are a few Chinese dishes (broccoli shrimp,
fried rice). But the real highlight is the *pho* (beef broth) and pork
dishes, like the house braised pork and lemongrass and mango
varieties. Beverage service is sketchy, so you may want to bring
your own bottle openers and glasses.
(773) 271-9828, phoxuarestaurant.com, Sun–Wed 10:30–10,
Thurs closed, Fri–Sat 10:30–11 🐝

PHOENIX INN $ / ★
608 Davis (Chicago), Evanston
Chinese
In business since 1970, new management recently took over this
downtown Evanston eatery and brightened up the small space
with bright green and yellow coats of paint. The menu still features standard Chinese fare, with plenty of vegetarian options and
Americanized standards (chop suey, fried rice, orange chicken).
(847) 475-7782, http://608phoenix.com, Mon–Thurs 11–9:30,
Fri–Sat 11–10, Sun 12–9:30 🐝

PINE YARD $$ / ★
1033 Davis (Oak), Evanston
Chinese
This elegant BYOB, which is just outside of downtown Evanston,
has been serving up Mandarin, Szechuan, and Cantonese cuisine
since 1973. BYOB isn't terribly common, but it is allowed, and
there's a decent wine shop just a couple of doors down.
(847) 475-4940, http://pineyardrestaurant.com, Mon–Fri
11:30–9:30, Sat 12–9:30, Sun 4:30–9:30 ⭐

PINTO THAI KITCHEN $ / ★
1931 Central (Green Bay), Evanston
Pan-Asian

Pinto's menu takes a stab at several Asian cuisines (Chinese,
Japanese, Thai) and offers updated versions of classic dishes like
Mongolian beef and Phuket noodle. There are also several dishes
you won't see elsewhere, like the soft-shell crab curry, asparagus
shrimp and scallops with oyster sauce, or mango and grilled
shrimp salad. Because they're focused on takeout and delivery, not
dine-in, service, beverage service is limited, but staff should be
able to provide a corkscrew and some water glasses on request.
(847) 328-8881, 11:30–9:30 daily ⊛

PIZZA ART CAFÉ $$ / ★★
4658 N. Rockwell (Eastwood), Ravenswood
Italian

Situated on a quaint street leading to one of the most beautiful
neighborhoods in the city, and just steps from the Rockwell stop
on the Brown Line, this cute, underrated 50-seat BYOB features
Neapolitan-influenced brick-oven pizzas, all topped with familiar
Italian ingredients (except for the house-cured smoked beef).
Pastas, antipasti, salads, and Italian entrées (lasagna, chicken
piccata) round out the rest of the menu.
(773) 539-0645, pizzaartcafe.info, Sun–Thurs 4:30–10, Fri–Sat
4:30–11 ⊛ 🐟

PIZZA BY ALEX $$ / ★★
5040–44 W. Montrose (Cicero), Northwest Side
Italian

Owner/chef Alex Pineda remodeled this former takeout-and-
delivery joint into a spacious dining room, complete with a
500-degree brick oven and bar (plans for a liquor license are
scrapped "for now"). Pineda serves homemade panini, panzerotti,
several Italian entrées, and two styles of pizza (Chicago-style and
brick-oven thin crust) so folks can debate which one's best.
(773) 427-8900, pizzabyalex.com, Mon–Thurs 10–10, Fri–Sat
10–12, Sun 11–10 ⊛

PIZZA RUSTICA $$ / ★★
3913 N. Sheridan (Dakin), Lakeview
Italian

Trendy thin-crust Italian pizzerias are the rage in Chicago, but this is one of the true originals. Pizza Rustica employs several Italian cooking methods to create their thin-crust, oven-baked, square-cut pizzas. But the heavenly pizzas aren't the only reason to trek to this BYOB. The pastas, salads, desserts, and daily specials (typically seafood and pasta entrées) represent rustic Italian at its finest. Wine glasses, ice buckets, and corkscrews are available on request.

(773) 404-8955, pizzarusticachicago.com, Sun–Mon 12–10, Tues closed, Wed–Thurs 12–10, Fri–Sat 12–11 ⚘ 🏴

PIZZERIA CALZONE $ / ★★
5858 N. Lincoln (Richmond), West Rogers Park
Italian

This neighborhood joint could have fallen into the takeout-and-delivery mold, but its spacious, remodeled dining room makes it a perfect BYOB for a casual night out when you're just too tired to cook. Grab a bottle of Italian wine, dive into a *margherita* pizza, and appreciate the savings. Corkage fee? Fuggedaboutit.

(773) 907-0917, Mon–Fri 10–12, Sat 10–12:30, Sun 10–11:30 🐡

POMEGRANATE $ / ★
1633 Orrington (Church), Evanston
Middle Eastern

Curiously, pomegranate isn't found anywhere on the menu. Irony aside, there is a nice mix of standard Middle Eastern fare (falafel, spinach pie, lentil soup, *fattoush*, chicken *shawerma*) and a couple of unique dishes, like the *mashwiya*, a dip made from zucchini, yogurt, garlic, and mint, or the *mo' jadara* plate, a vegetarian dish of lentils, rice, caramelized onions, and yogurt. Other than providing a corkscrew and some ice, no beverage service is available.

(847) 475-6002, eatpom.com, Mon–Sat 11–10, Sun 12–9 🐡

POT PAN $ / ★★
1362 N. Milwaukee (Wood), Wicker Park
Thai

Now that they've moved from North and Wood to this new location, business has really picked up, especially on the weekends. Pot Pan's menu hasn't changed; the same variety of Thai noodle dishes, curries, and appetizers are available, all served in an updated space with Asian-inspired decor. Corkage fee is waived with order of one entrée per person.

(773) 862-6990, potpanthai.com, Mon–Thurs 11–10, Fri–Sat 11–11, Sun 12–10

P.S. BANGKOK 2 $ / ★★
2521 N. Halsted (Lill), Lincoln Park
Thai

Trendy bars and eateries come and go in this area, but P.S. Bangkok 2 has served traditional Thai fare for 25 years and counting. (The owner's sister runs the original P.S. Bangkok in Lakeview, which has a liquor license but allows BYOB for a $10 corkage fee.) If recent improvements are any indication—the decor received a facelift and the menu now features seasonal specials such as coconut puffs, tamarind noodles, and spicy sesame noodles—they'll be around for 25 more.

(773) 348-0072, psbangkok2.com, Mon–Thurs 11–10, Fri–Sat 11:30–11, Sun 4:30–10 ☻

QUANG $ / ★
804 N. State (Chicago), Near North
Thai/Vietnamese

There aren't many casual Vietnamese places in this neck of the woods, but this mostly takeout and delivery joint obliges with dishes such as fried catfish, *pho*, and lemongrass chicken. A comprehensive Thai menu is available, as well.

(312) 951-9030, Mon–Sat 11–9 (closed 3–5), Sun closed ☻

RADHUNI $$ / ★★★
3227 N. Clark (Belmont), Lakeview
Indian

Surprisingly, there are few Indian eateries left in Lakeview, so
Radhuni ("home cooked") is a welcome addition to the area,
offering a promising menu of Northern and Southeastern Indian
cuisine. Prepared by a chef trained in UK-based Indian cuisine,
the dishes use slightly different ingredients (no tomato paste,
yogurt, or curry flour) and spices are all made on-site. You'll
find all the Indian staples (tandoori, samosa, tikka masala) and
a lunch-only daily buffet. Beer mugs, wine glasses, Champagne
flutes, ice buckets, and corkscrews are available on request.
(773) 404-5670, Mon–Thurs 11–10, Fri–Sun 11–10:30 ⊛

RANALLI'S OF ANDERSONVILLE $$ / ★★
1512 W. Berwyn (Ashland), Andersonville
Italian

Open since 2007, this remodeled, loft-like space offers a casual
place to dine on fresh Italian food without doing too much
damage to your wallet. There's a wide mix of sandwiches (panini,
Italian beef, Angus burgers), pastas (ravioli, lasagna), appetizers
(fried calamari, antipasti platter), ribs, steak, and salads. Not
to mention their trademark pizzas—five styles in all—with no
charge for more than four ingredients. A liquor license application
was in the works at press time, but corkage-free BYOB dining will
still be welcome even if it's approved.
(773) 334-1300, ranallispizza.com, Sun–Thurs 11–11, Fri–Sat
11–12 ⊛ ✒

RAPA NUI $$ / ★★
4009 N. Elston (Irving), Albany Park
Chilean

Owners changed the name (formerly Latin Sandwich) and
swapped the sandwich menu for traditional Chilean cuisine,
giving the small dining room a Polynesian makeover along the
way. The resulting Rapa Nui (regional name for Easter Island)
now serves *parrilladas*, or tabletop grill, steaks, seafood, and a
few items from the old menu, like the empanadas and Cuban
sandwich. No hard alcohol allowed.
(773) 478-0175, rapanuichicago.com, Mon–Tues 11–5, Wed–
Thurs 11–10, Fri–Sat 11–11, Sun 1–9 ✒

REAL AZTECA $$ / ★
5661 N. Clark (Hollywood), Edgewater
Mexican

Along with plates of fajitas, chile rellenos, and *chilaquiles* is a
surprisingly ambitious rotating menu of contemporary American
and Latin-influenced appetizers, entrées, and desserts. Find pork
tenderloin with sweet potatoes, ginger shrimp, baby spinach
salad, whitefish with couscous and mole sauce, and *tres leches*
gelato. Space is pretty tight and beverage service is limited, but
they may be able to scare up a wine glass or two.
(773) 516-4913, Mon–Wed 11–9, Thurs–Sat 11–10, Sun 10–6 ⊗

REAL TENOCHTITLAN $$$$ / ★★★★
2451 N. Milwaukee (Sacramento), Logan Square
Nuevo Latino

Geno Bahena (Los Moles, Frontera Grill, Topolobampo, Tepatul-
co) sold this place in spring 2009 but left a permanent imprint on
the menu with items like his trademark mole sauces (see the Web
site for daily specials). A liquor license application has been in the
works since 2008, so it's anyone's guess how long this place will
remain BYOB. In the meantime, they offer nonalcoholic sangrita
mix and will whip up freshly made pitchers of virgin margarita
mix, complete with garnished margarita glasses, to blend with
your tequila. Wine glasses, pilsner glasses, shot glasses, ice
buckets, and corkscrews are also available upon request.
(773) 227-1050, realtenochtitlan.com, Mon–Thurs 11:30–2:30,
5–10, Fri–Sat 10:30–2:30, 5–11, Sun 10–2:30, reservations
recommended ⊗ ♥

RESTAURANT SARAJEVO $$ / ★★★
2701 W. Lawrence (Washtenaw), Ravenswood
Bosnian

When Enes Hubjer decided to open this restaurant in 1999
without a liquor license, "BYOB" was not in his vocabulary. But
ever since wine connoisseurs and budget foodies have found this
newly christened BYOB, business is better than ever. In an elegant
dining room, regulars feast on homemade Bosnian beef sausage,
grilled mushrooms, and *cevapcici* (seasoned ground beef on
homemade lepina bread). White and red wine glasses, Champagne flutes, ice buckets, and corkscrews are available on request.
(773) 275-5310, restaurantsarajevo.com, 9–10 daily ⤧

RICE THAI $ / ★
6744 N. Sheridan (Pratt), Rogers Park
Thai
Located next door to the newly remodeled Village Theater, Rice
Thai offers the usual variety of Thai quick bites (chicken satay,
tom kha, pad Thai, curries, ginger catfish) and a handful of maki
rolls. There are only a few tables inside, but a busy outdoor patio
brings this place to life in warmer months.
(773) 338-1717, Mon–Thurs 11–9:30, Fri–Sat 11–10, Sun
12–9:30 🛇 🖈

ROBINSON'S NO. 1 RIBS LINCOLN PARK $$ / ★★
655 W. Armitage (Orchard), Lincoln Park
BBQ
Founder Charlie Robinson is famous for his award-winning ribs,
which took first place at Mike Rokyo's Ribfest in 1982 and several
cook-offs since. Robinson's franchises are now independently
owned and operated, and this is the only one that's BYOB. Baby
back ribs are dry-rubbed, hickory smoked on-site, then served
with one of Robinson's famous sauces (brown sugar, hot sauce, or
the original). A large outdoor space, which accommodates up to
40, is popular for private parties.
(312) 337-1399, ribs1.com, Mon closed, Tues–Thurs 11–9, Fri
11–10, Sat 4–10, Sun 3–8 🛇 🖈

ROLIS RESTAURANT $$ / ★★★
5004 N. Sheridan (Argyle), Uptown
Mexican/Brunch
Husband-wife team Jose and Rosie Tenoryo took over this storefront BYOB (formerly Rique's), naming their first venture after
their son. Everything is made in-house, including the guacamole,
pico de gallo, chicken with red mole, and, for the undecided, five
different combo plates. Margarita and wine glasses are available
on request, and a private party room in back seats about 30.
(773) 728-6200, Sun–Thurs 10–10, Fri–Sat 10–11 🛇 🍸

ROONG PETCH $ / ★★
1828 W. Montrose (Ravenswood), Ravenswood
Japanese/Thai
A recent remodeling job spruced up the atmosphere at this
neighborhood Thai joint (after 21 years, it was time). Along with
new lighting fixtures and a fresh coat of lavender paint, owner
Chariya Sopanarat also added a sushi bar, which is only available
at dinner. A liquor store down the block has upgraded its offerings in case you find yourself empty-handed.
(773) 989-0818, roongpetch.com, Mon–Thurs 11:30–9:30,
Fri–Sat 11:30–10, Sun closed ⊛

ROSATI'S $$ / -
126 W. Grand (LaSalle), River North
Italian
The menu choices are dizzying: entrées, 50 different types of
salads and sandwiches (at co-venture California Style Deli), and
Rosati's trademark thin-crust pizza. But wait, there's more: double
dough, deep dish, and stuffed pizzas; desserts from Eli's and
Sugar & Spice; panzerotti (folded and stuffed pizza); sides; and
starters. But no beverage service is available, so BYO bottle opener
and glasses.
(312) 755-9955, californiastyledeli.com, Sun–Thurs 10–10, Fri–Sat
10–11 ⊛ ⏀ Ⓟ

ROSDED $ / ★
2308 W. Leland (Lincoln), Lincoln Square
Thai
Not many places can claim they've been in business since
1976—especially in gentrified neighborhoods such as Lincoln
Square. But Rosded is one of these, with regulars filling the small
dining room at all hours of the day and night. Diners don't BYOB
at this family-oriented place as much as they do at others in the
area, but it is welcome.
(773) 334-9055, Mon closed, Tues–Sat 11:30–9, Sun 12–8:30 ⊛

ROYAL THAI $ / ★★
2209 W. Montrose (Lincoln), Lincoln Square
Thai

Fresh flowers at each table, hypnotic background music, and a
resident fish tank give this family-run place a relaxed vibe. Just
a few steps from the bustle of Lincoln Avenue near Welles Park,
Royal Thai offers nearly 100 menu items, most of the classic Thai
variety, but several house specials set it apart, like the wonton and
Royal Thai prawns.

(773) 509-0007, royalthaichicago.com, Mon–Thurs 11:30–9:30,
Fri–Sat 11:30–10:30, Sun 12–9:30 ⊛

RUBY OF SIAM $$ / ★★
9420 Skokie Blvd. (Golf), Skokie
Thai

Located in the Fashion Square Mall, Ruby of Siam has been a
Skokie mainstay for over 10 years. Faced with their overwhelm-
ing menu of over 100 choices, you may be tempted to default
to safe bets like pad Thai and satay. But use the opportunity to
go outside your comfort zone with dishes like *pad ped pladook*
(catfish sautéed with red curry, eggplant, and sweet basil) or the
nam sod (a cold salad of minced broiled chicken or pork with
lime, hot peppers, and peanuts).

(847) 675-7008, rubyofsiam.com, Mon–Thurs 11–10, Fri–Sat
11–11, Sun 12–10 ⊛ Ⓟ

RUBY OF SIAM $ / ★
170 W. Washington (LaSalle), the Loop
Thai

This 80-seat sister location offers the same menu to the business
lunch and dinner crowd.

(312) 609-0000, rubyofsiam.com, Mon–Fri 10:30–9, Sat 12–10,
Sun 12–9 ⊛

SABAI DEE $ / ★
5359 N. Broadway (Balmoral), Andersonville
Lao
Sabai Dee, which apparently translates to "hello, how are you?"
is a modern, 22-seat, sunny spot that serves updated versions
of Lao fare (*pho* Lao, green papaya salad), which overlaps with
other types of Southeastern Asian cuisine. There are far superior
Asian joints in the surrounding area, so stick with safe bets, like
their noodle soups. Or, just pick up your dinner at the adjoining
Golden Pacific Market, an amazing Asian grocery.
(773) 506-0880, sabaidee-chicago.com, Mon closed, Tues–Sun
10:30–9 ☺

SABOR A CUBA $$ / ★★
1833 W. Wilson (Wolcott), Ravenswood
Cuban
Sabor A Cuba is a quintessential neighborhood ethnic eatery,
serving traditional Cuban cuisine in a family-friendly atmosphere
(but with enough ambience for a dinner date or celebratory
night out). The menu comprises a full range of traditional Cuban
favorites, such as *lechon asado* (marinated rotisserie pork) and *ropa
vieja* (shredded beef in a Cuban sauce). Mixers on their menu are
not allowed (i.e., cola, which they are happy to blend with some
limes and your bottle of rum for a batch of *Cuba libre*).
(773) 769-6859, saboracubachicago.com, Mon closed,
Tues–Thurs 11–10, Fri–Sat 12–11, Sun 11–9, reservations
recommended ☺ 🍴

SABOR MICHOACÁN $$ / ★
7021 N. Clark (Lunt), Rogers Park
Mexican
The brightly painted walls and counter service give Sabor
Michoacán ("taste of Michoacán," a Mexican state) a vibe that's
half small-town diner, half taqueria. But make no mistake; this is
not your average takeout joint. Expect steaks, seafood, traditional
Mexican eats (chile rellenos, gorditas), and a full breakfast menu.
(773) 465-1122, 10–11 daily ☺

SAHARA KABOB $$ / ★★
6649 N. Clark (Wallen), Rogers Park
Middle Eastern
This place may have lost some of its charm with a name change (formerly Big Buns and Pita), but the made-to-order Assyrian cuisine and friendly staff are two reasons to keep coming back. Health-conscious diners will appreciate the menu, with choices like bulgur wheat couscous, chicken kibbeh, and delish appetizers like *lahmim beajin*, a Mediterranean pizza with ground beef, spices, tomatoes, onions, parsley.
(773) 262-2000, saharakabob.com, Sun–Thurs 11–10, Fri–Sat 11–11 ⊛

SAN CHAE DOL SOT RESTAURANT $$ / ★★★
3737B W. Lawrence (Ridgeway), Albany Park
Korean
If the true test of a restaurant's authenticity is the ethnicity of its customers, then this place passes with flying colors. Expect authentic Korean fare like kimchee, *bulgogi,* hot pots, and *bee-bim bop* served in a family-friendly setting. Beer mugs, Korean wine glasses (yes, there is such a thing), and rocks glasses are available on request. $20 credit card minimum.
(773) 588-5223, Mon–Sat 10:30–10:30, Sun closed ⊛ Ⓟ

SAPORE DI NAPOLI $$ / ★★
1406 W. Belmont (Southport), Lakeview
Italian
Owners have really focused on the details at this 30-seat neighborhood spot, which features a rustic Italian menu using authentic ingredients. The flour, prosciutto, oil, and mozzarella are all imported from Naples, and the house specialty 12-inch thin-crust pizzas (there are almost 20 selections, and each serves 1–2 people), are baked in an imported 800-degree brick oven. Pastas, antipasti, salads, and rotating flavors of gelato round out the menu.
(773) 935-1212, saporedinapoli.net, Mon closed, Tues–Sat 4–11, Sun 4–10 ⊛

SATAY $$ / ★★
936 W. Diversey (Wilton), Lakeview
Pan-Asian
Located next to the Brown Line's Diversey stop, this place offers
a wide mix of Chinese, Japanese, and Thai dishes. Choose from
more mainstream fare like pad Thai and fried rice, or lemon
honey spicy chicken and chicken and mango for more adventurous options. The combination meals are a true bargain: For
around $12, you get a choice of entrée, spring roll or California
maki roll, soup, salad, and rice. A back room accommodates
parties up to 50.
(773) 477-0100, Sun–Mon 4–10, Tues–Thurs 11–10, Fri–Sat
11–11 ⊛ ⏏

SCHWA $$$$ / ★
1466 N. Ashland (LeMoyne), Wicker Park
Eclectic
Chef/owner Michael Carlson and Grant Achatz worked together
at Trio before embarking on their own ventures. Achatz, of
course, opened Alinea, and Carlson went his own way to head up
this 26-seat storefront spot. Though the two chefs offer innova-
tive haute cuisine, their approaches couldn't be further apart.
At Schwa, Carlson plays multiple roles as host, chef, and server,
while his small staff assists with the rotating three-course ($55) or
nine-course ($110) menus. Though the courses change season-
ally or at whim, mainstays include the quail egg ravioli, a house
specialty, and a peeky toe crab *jibarito*. Other dishes play with
unlikely savory/sweet combinations, like green curry and root
beer maki, or rabbit with peaches, wheatgrass, and Gumballhead
beer. Presentation plays a large part in the dining experience; a
dish might include grapefruit segments with honey sorbet and
chamomile perched on a glass cube, and flavors are introduced
via foams and shavings. Schwa's unpredictable reservation system,
loud music, and unconventional schedule make it the punk
rocker of haute cuisine in Chicago. When considering what wines
to bring, stick with food-friendly, high-acid, medium-bodied
wines that will cleanse your palate and pair with most foods, like
sparkling dry rosé, pinot gris, pinot noir, or brut Champagne.
Best bet? Bring several bottles of wine (or beer, wheat beers
should work well) and experiment to see what works.
(773) 252-1466, schwarestaurant.com, Sun–Mon closed, Tues–Sat
5:30–10:30, reservations required ⏏

SEMIRAMIS $$ / ★★
4639–41 N. Kedzie (Eastwood), Albany Park
Middle Eastern
This area is saturated with Middle Eastern eateries, but most of
them fall in the super-casual or takeout-joint categories. And
while many are simply BYOB by default, chef/owner Joseph
Abraham's spot has always been BYOB by design, as he chooses
to focus on delicious, made-to-order Lebanese cuisine instead of a
full bar. You can't go wrong with any of the Middle Eastern staples
on the menu (falafel, kebabs, tabouleh), but the tender chicken
shawerma, wrapped in light pita bread and dressed in homemade
tahini sauce, is one of the safest bets.
(773) 279-8900, semiramisrestaurant.com, Mon–Thurs 11–10,
Fri–Sat 11–11, Sun closed ☺

SEVEN TREASURES $$ / -
2312 S. Wentworth (23rd), Chinatown
Chinese
Located in the heart of Chinatown since 1985, this BYOB is
blocked from holding a liquor license because of its proximity to
the church across the street. The specialty here is Hong Kong–
style BBQ chicken, which is marinated, roasted, then sold by the
pound (pork and duck are also available). If BBQ isn't your thing,
aim for the reliable orange chicken or fried pork chops.
(312) 225-2668, seventreasures.com, 11–2a daily ☺

SHER-A-PUNJAB $$ / ★★
2510 W. Devon (Maplewood), West Rogers Park
Indian
All-you-can-eat buffets don't normally conjure up visions of
high-quality, freshly prepared food. Sher-A-Punjab is out to
change that. Their lunch and dinner buffets, which go for less
than 10 bucks a head, are prepared fresh daily and without oil, so
dishes don't sit around in unappetizing pools of grease. Choose
from flaky samosas, butter chicken, masala dosa, chicken *biryani*,
and more. Or, order from the menu, which offers a full range of
Northern and Southern Indian cuisine.
(773) 973-4000, 11–11 daily, reservations recommended on
weekends ☺

SHINOBU $$$ / ★★
1131 W. Bryn Mawr (Winthrop), Edgewater
Japanese
Located in the reclaimed Bryn Mawr Historic District, this
contemporary spot serves reasonably priced sushi and traditional
Japanese kitchen fare (teriyaki, udon, katsu, gyoza). A former
Arun's chef is behind the sushi bar, preparing signature rolls like
the black spider, a creation of soft-shell crab, eel, cream cheese,
cucumber, and tempura crumbs. If you're looking for an unpretentious yet modern sushi bar on the North Side, this is the place.
(773) 334-9062, shinoburestaurant.com, Mon–Sat 12–10, Sun
4–10 🕸

SHISO $$ / ★★★
449 W. North (Cleveland), Old Town
Japanese
This newish spot (owned by Tony Kammaty, brother of BYOB
Blue Elephant owner Tommy Kammaty) serves a full menu of
Japanese appetizers, entrées, teriyakis, soups, and sushi in a sleek,
contemporary setting. Shiso (Japanese term for a leafy green) also
has a few offbeat dishes, like the *takoyaki* (baked octopus puffs)
and *donburi*, a popular Japanese dish served over bowls of rice.
Beer glasses, wine glasses, sake cups, corkscrews, and ice buckets
are available on request.
(312) 649-1234, shisochicago.com, 11–10 daily 🕸

SHOKOLAD $ / ★★
2524 W. Chicago (Maplewood), West Town
Eclectic/Brunch
Halyna Fedus, a former pastry chef at local Limelight Catering, is
behind this neighborhood café. Though the decor and parts of the
menu draw from Italian influences, from the panini sandwiches
to the pastries to the Caffe Umbria coffee, Ukrainian fare takes
up most of the menu. For starters there are potato pancakes and
borscht, and for main courses *varenykui* (Ukrainian pierogies),
pelmeni (pork wrapped in pastry dough), beef Stroganoff, roast
duck, and pork chops. Breakfast choices include omelettes and
sweet or savory crepes.
(773) 276-6402, Mon–Fri 9–6, Sat–Sun 9–5 🕸 🏴

SHOKRAN MOROCCAN GRILL $$ / ★★
4027 W. Irving Park (Pulaski), Irving Park
Moroccan
This place was the Blue Line Bakery, which sold Moroccan treats to a steady stream of commuters. But customers clamored for a full-service restaurant, so owner Khali Kamal changed the name and added a full lunch and dinner menu. He draped the two back rooms in Moroccan tapestries and added some mood lighting for a slightly romantic, but still casual, atmosphere. Expect couscous entrées, tagines (Moroccan stews), and kebabs.
(773) 427-9130, 11–10 daily ⊛

SHUI WAH $$ / ★
2162A S. Archer (Cermak), Chinatown
Chinese
Open since 1999, Shui Wah serves dim sum from 8–3 every day. The most popular choices are the steamed shrimp, pork, chicken, spare ribs, and chicken feet with black bean dumplings. Sweeter options include the egg-yolk cream roll or mango pudding varieties. There's also a dinner-only menu featuring *chow chiu* cooking, or Hong Kong–style cuisine.
(312) 225-8811, 8–3 (dim sum), 4–2a (dinner) daily ⊛

SIAM CAFÉ $ / ★★
4712 N. Sheridan (Leland), Uptown
Thai
When the city of Chicago initiated a two-year requirement for its on-premise liquor licenses, Siam Café—one of Chicago's oldest Thai restaurants—gave up their bar and adopted a BYOB policy. Enjoy a wide variety of authentic Thai dishes, from curries and pad Thai to cuttlefish salad and red snapper. A wide variety of glassware is available, left over from their full-service bar.
(773) 769-6602, Wed–Mon 11:30–9, Tues closed ⌔

SIAM COUNTRY $ / ★★
4637 N. Damen (Eastwood), Ravenswood
Thai

Located just steps from the Damen stop on the Brown Line, this
family-style eatery was the first restaurant on the block when it
opened (the current owner bought it from her mother in 1992).
Now this quaint area boasts several cafés, bars, and BYOBs.
There's a ban on liquor licenses at this address, but the liquor
store just a few doors down stocks microbrews and boutique
wines if you're empty-handed.
(773) 271-0700, siamcountrychicago.com, Sun–Tues 11:30–9:30,
Wed closed, Thurs 11:30–9:30, Fri–Sat 11:30–10 ✪ 🏴

SIAM NOODLE & RICE $ / ★★
4654 N. Sheridan (Wilson), Uptown
Thai

Low-key, traditional Thai eateries seem to flourish on this block.
In business in 1987, this family owned and operated neighborhood spot specializes in homestyle cooking. All of the sauces
(peanut, plum, ginger) and curries are made in-house, and the
varied menu avoids run-of-the-mill status. Don't go from 4–5;
they're closed for the daily family sit-down meal. (Bring a chilled
bottle if you want to avoid the fee for ice.)
(773) 769-6694, siamnoodleandrice.com, Mon closed,
Tues–Thurs 11–9, Fri 11–9:30, Sat 11:30–9:30, Sun 11:30–8
(closed daily from 4–5) ✪

SIAM RICE THAI CUISINE $ / ★★
117 N. Wells (Washington), the Loop
Thai

Named after a staple in the Thai diet (also referred to as jasmine
rice), Siam Rice Thai Cuisine features a sleek, 100-seat dining
room, with cherrywood walls, limestone tiles, and contemporary
lighting, offering a refreshing alternative to typical lunch and
dinner choices in the Loop. It's close to the Theater District, and
the quick service will help you make it to your show on time.
(312) 606-9999, siamricethai.com, Mon–Fri 11–8, Sat–Sun
closed ✪

SIAM TASTE NOODLE $ / ★★
4323 W. Addison (Milwaukee), Old Irving Park
Thai

Because of a state ordinance that prohibits businesses from
selling alcohol near K–12 schools (the restaurant is kitty-corner
from Schurz High School), Siam Taste Noodle is permanently
BYOB. Chef/owner Renoo Ranumas, who honed her culinary
skills for the past 30 years in both Thailand and the United
States, prepares healthy Thai dishes using only vegetable oils and
no MSG (and she isn't afraid to make it spicy). Any dish can be
adapted for vegetarians.
(773) 286-6020, siamtaste.info, Mon–Sat 11–10, Sun 12–10 ⊛

SIKIA $$$ / ★★
740 W. 63rd (Halsted), South Side
African/Brunch

Sikia ("harmony" in Swahili) is the second restaurant run by the
faculty and students of Washburne Culinary Institute (Parrot
Cage is the other). Drawing on the diverse cuisines within Africa,
students prepare ambitious dishes such as Northern African
tilapia, grilled rib eye with *harissa* sauce, Senegalese peanut soup,
black-eyed pea fritters, and seasonal desserts from Washburne's
French Pastry School. A piano fills the elegant dining room with
live music on Thursday nights.
(773) 602-5200, Mon–Wed closed, Thurs–Sat 5:30–9:30, Sun
11–3 ⌇

SIMPLY IT $$ / ★★
2269 N. Lincoln (Belden), Lincoln Park
Vietnamese

Owner Tuan Nguyen (Pasteur, Viet Bistro) and chef Hung Hoang
(Le Colonial) offer a modified version of Vietnamese fine-dining
at this casual, 56-seat BYOB. Entrées hover around $14 and
represent a full spectrum of Vietnamese cuisine, from lemongrass
chicken to spare ribs to catfish in a clay pot, using only fresh,
seasonal ingredients and authentic Thai seasonings. Validated
parking is available at Children's Memorial Hospital for about $6.
(773) 248-0884, simplyitrestaurant.com, Mon closed, Tues–Thurs
11–10, Fri–Sat 11–11, Sun 12–10 ⊛

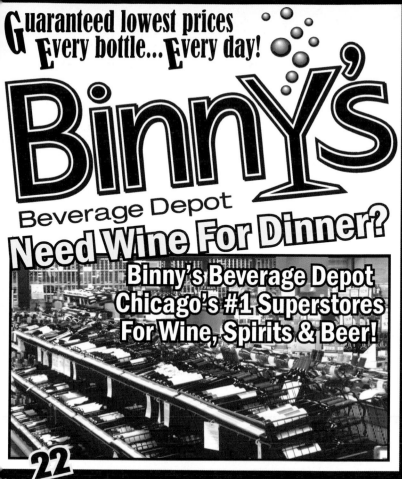

Gifts

Clubs

Events

Parties

Discover

In Fine Spirits, Chicago's world of wine, spirits and microbrews, where "fine" and "fun" don't have to be mutually exclusive. Located in Andersonville our shop and bar of the same name specialize in new world wine, unusual varietals, artisan spirits and craft beers that represent the cutting-edge of quality and value. A spirit of adventure awaits you with our friendly and knowledgeable staff ready to guide you in your exploration.

IN FINE SPIRITS

SMAK TAK $$ / ★★
5961 N. Elston (Austin), Northwest Side
Polish

This cozy, authentic Polish spot has been enjoying a cult following ever since word of its BYOB status got out. Enjoy hearty fare like traditional pierogi, Polish sausage, potato pancakes, and stuffed cabbage. Street parking is still free in this part of the city (as of press time, anyway).

(773) 763-1123, smaktak.com, 11–9 daily ⊛

SMOKE SHACK $$ / -
800 W. Altgeld (Halsted), Lincoln Park
BBQ

Smoke Shack's menu represents several regional BBQ styles (Carolina, Texas, St. Louis), even an Argentinian smoked chorizo with *chimichurri* sauce, and sauces and rubs are made in-house. The "Taste of Smoke Shack" is probably the best deal, consisting of two St. Louis ribs, two baby back ribs, half of a pulled pork sandwich, half of a brisket sandwich, and the aforementioned chorizo for about $16. Comfort food sides like mac and cheese and mashed potatoes are also available. There may be a bottle opener around, but otherwise beverage service—like the atmosphere—is lacking.

(773) 248-8886, smokeshackchicago.com, Mon closed, Tues–Wed 11–9, Thurs 11–2a, Fri–Sat 11–4a, Sun 11–9 ⊛

SMOQUE BBQ $$ / ★
3800 N. Pulaski (Grace), Old Irving Park
BBQ

Every neighborhood seems to have its resident BBQ joint, and Old Irving Park is no exception. Slow-smoked meats and homemade comfort-food sides are the order of the day at this enormously popular joint, which offers a hybrid of BBQ styles. Even though nearby residents deterred Smoque's liquor *and* patio licenses, it hasn't kept a loyal following from packing this place for the Texas brisket, Memphis ribs, pulled pork, and mac and cheese. Grab a plastic cup, some red zinfandel, and dig in.

(773) 545-7427, smoquebbq.com, Mon closed, Tues–Thurs 11–9, Fri–Sat 11–10, Sun 11–9 ⊛

SNAIL THAI CUISINE $ / ★★★
1649 E. 55th (Hyde Park Blvd.), Hyde Park
Thai

No, you won't find any snails on the menu. You will find *sai krok e-sarn* (Northeastern Thai–style sausages with ginger, green chili, and roasted peanuts) and other dishes, which have attracted a following to Marisa Suriyavong's 80-seat eatery since 1993. They're generous with beverage service, providing chilled beer mugs and red and white wine glasses on request.
(773) 667-5423, snailthai.com, Mon closed, Tues–Sun 11–10 ⊛

SO GONG DONG TOFU RESTAURANT $ / ★
3307 W. Bryn Mawr (Kedzie), North Park
Korean

The specialty at this long-standing neighborhood eatery is the extensive variety of tofu-based soups, but there are also Korean classics like steamed dumplings, hot pots, Korean pancakes, and *bee-bim bop*. They will provide water glasses and corkscrews on request.
(773) 539-8377, Thurs–Mon 10–10, Wed closed ⊛

THE SPICE FUSION $–$$ / ★★
THAI & JAPANESE CUISINE
2886 N. Milwaukee (Allen), Logan Square
Japanese/Thai

Like so many other Thai BYOBs in town, The Spice added a sushi bar recently to change with the times. Now the menu is split evenly between Thai and Japanese cuisine, and the decor has been updated for a more contemporary look. Wine glasses, corkscrews, and ice buckets are available on request.
(773) 252-9959, thespicechicago.com. Sun–Mon 4–10, Tues–Fri 11–10, Sat 11:30–10 ⊛

SPOON THAI $ / ★★
4608 N. Western (Wilson), Lincoln Square
Thai

Though there are several Thai eateries within a block of this place, none seems to be suffering from the competition. In fact, business is booming. In Spoon's case, credit a menu that continues to expand with traditional Thai fare like Northern Thai sausage, banana blossom salad, and catfish in curry sauce.
(773) 769-1173, spoonthai.com, 11–10 daily ⊛

SPRING WORLD $$ / ★
2109A S. China Place (Cermak), Chinatown
Chinese
This small, charming spot is located in the heart of the Chinatown
Square, an open-air plaza of restaurants, bakeries, grocery shops,
and offices. The menu draws upon influences throughout the
Orient but is primarily focused on Yunan cuisine, like the "rice
noodle across bridge" special or rice noodle soup.
(312) 326-9966, Mon–Thurs 11–10, Fri 10:30–10, Sat–Sun
10–10 ⊛

STAGES $ / ★
657 W. 31st (Union), Bridgeport
American
There's something for everyone at this casual, family-friendly,
150-seat diner: burgers, hearty deli sandwiches, stir-fry, steaks,
Greek dishes—even Weight Watchers–approved options for
dieters. Breakfast (skillets, omelettes, steak and eggs, French
toast) is served all day. BYOB is not terribly common here, but it
is allowed.
(312) 225-0396, 6–9 daily ✧

STANDARD INDIA $$ / ★★
917 W. Belmont (Clark), Lakeview
Indian
Regulars have been coming here since 1988 for the lunch and
dinner buffets ($9.95 and $10.95, respectively), but a solid menu
of Northern Indian cuisine is available as well. Fill up on clay
oven specialties (tandoori, tikka), lamb (*rogan josh*, vindaloo)
biryanis (rice dishes), and several vegetarian options (*saag paneer*,
channa masala). There are also several freshly baked breads (naan,
roti) to nosh on with your own wine or beer.
(773) 929-1123, standardindianrestaurant.com, lunch: 12–3
daily; dinner: Sun–Thurs 5–10, Fri–Sat 5–11 ⊛

STAR OF INDIA $ / ★
3204 N. Sheffield (Belmont), Lakeview
Indian

The in-house tandoor (clay oven) at this long-standing Lakeview eatery produces all sorts of Indian fare, from shish kebabs to chicken, fish, and lamb entrées. There are also 10 homemade breads to choose from, as well as a wide variety of vegetarian and meat-based curries. Lunch and dinner buffets are available daily for under $10.

(773) 525-2100, Sun–Thurs 11:30–10, Fri–Sat 11:30–11 ⊛

STICKY RICE $ / ★★
4018 N. Western (Irving Park), North Center
Thai

This restaurant's namesake is the type of rice found in Northern Thailand (instead of jasmine rice), where it's used like bread and eaten with the hands. Enjoy it here with finger-food dishes like *nam prik ong, nam prik nhum,* and *larb.* This place is also known for its handmade *sai ma,* or Northern Thai sausage, made with pork sausage, lemongrass, lime, and red curry. There is a separate Thai menu with an English translation.

(773) 588-0133, stickyricethai.com, Mon–Sat 11:30–11, Sun 12–10 ⊛ ✈

SULTAN'S MARKET $ / -
2057 W. North (Hoyne), Wicker Park
Middle Eastern

When this place opened, people lined up daily for the cheap falafel sandwiches in Soup Nazi–fashion. Sultan's has since expanded with a grocery store, salad bar ($5.99 per pound), and a remodeled dining area. There's still a line, but now it's for falafel, *shawerma,* lentil soup, and more. BYOB isn't too common at either location, but it is allowed (and you better bring your own corkscrew or bottle opener).

(773) 235-3072, chicagofalafel.com, Mon–Sat 10–9, Sun 10–7 ⊛ ✈

SULTAN'S MARKET $ / -
2521 N. Clark (Deming), Lincoln Park
Middle Eastern
This outpost is quite a bit smaller than the original Wicker Park
location, but it offers the same menu (without the salad bar).
(312) 638-9151, chicagofalafel.com, Mon–Thurs 10–10, Fri–Sat
10–12, Sun 10–9 ✪

SUMMER NOODLE & RICE $$ / ★★
1123 W. Granville (Kenmore), Edgewater
Pan-Asian
This neighborhood spot offers the usual Chinese and Thai
noodle and rice suspects, but there are plenty of off-the-beaten-
path options to spice things up. Try the smoked chili noodles,
gado-gado (Thai-Indonesian dish with shrimp, tofu, bean sprouts,
and peanut sauce), spicy mango shrimp, Bangkok street calamari
(grilled calamari and asparagus with chili lime sauce), or summer
tempura (sweet potato tempura with Japanese BBQ sauce).
(773) 761-8500, summerchicago.com, Mon–Sat 11:30–10, Sun
12–9 ✪

SUNSHINE CAFÉ $ / -
5449 N. Clark (Catalpa), Andersonville
Japanese
This low-key neighborhood place specializes in homestyle
Japanese cooking, so there's no sushi bar or contemporary cuisine
on the menu. But that's not a bad thing. Sunshine's specialty is
udon noodle soup, the Japanese version of Vietnamese *pho*. For
less than 10 bucks, get an enormous bowl of broth filled with
noodles, vegetables, and choice of meat (leftovers guaranteed).
Management asks that BYOB customers don't arrive near closing
time. Family place, y'all.
(773) 334-6214, Mon closed, Tues–Sun 12–9 ✪

SUSHI MON $$ / ★★
2441 N. Clark (Fullerton), Lincoln Park
Japanese
Sushi chef Bat Mashigjav took over the Sushi & Deli space in
2008, performed a makeover, and now claims that it's the only
place in Chicago serving "pressed sushi," in which the rice and ingredients that go into each piece of sushi or maki are compressed
then topped with avocado, raw fish, and sauce. The 20-seat eatery
caters mostly to takeout and delivery customers, but they have a
handful of wine glasses and sake cups on hand for BYOB diners.
(773) 529-8812, sushimonchicago.com, Mon–Thurs 11–9:30, Fri
11–11, Sat 12–11, Sun 4–9 ☕

SUSHI 28 CAFÉ $–$$$ / ★★★
2863 N. Clark (Diversey), Lakeview
Japanese/Vietnamese
If you're looking for a noodle shop or sushi bar before heading to
Lakeview bars or the nearby Landmark's Century Centre theater,
this place hits both marks (just look for the empty wine and sake
bottles in the front window). There's a surprising selection of Vietnamese dishes at this tiny eatery (vermicelli noodle bowls, *pho*,
lemongrass chicken) as well as dozens of sushi and maki options,
fashioned by Peninsula-vet/sushi chef Sally Kwok. Wine glasses,
sake cups, even Champagne flutes are available on request.
(773) 868-1250, sushi28cafe.com, Sun–Mon 12:30–10, Tues
closed, Wed–Thurs 12:30–10, Fri–Sat 12–10:30 ☕

SUSHI II PARA $$$ / ★★★
2256 N. Clark (Belden), Lincoln Park
Japanese
This low-key, traditional sushi spot has doubled in size with an
upstairs seating area for up to 70 people (yet another sign that
BYOB business has grown during the economic downtown).
The specialty here is all-you-can-eat sushi, available for less than
$20. There's also teriyaki, Japanese appetizers and soups, and a
full sushi menu. Staff will provide sake cups, beer glasses, wine
glasses, and ice buckets on request.
(773) 477-3219, Mon–Thurs 11–10, Fri–Sat 11–10:30, Sun
12:30–9:30 ☕

SUSHI X $$$ / ★
1136 W. Chicago (Racine), River West
Japanese
This original location (the Lakeview offspring has a liquor license)
offers only maki rolls, no sushi, but the high-quality fish and
inventive combinations place it several notches above other maki
around town. The dimly lit, stark dining room has an intimate,
lounge-like atmosphere, with Japanese *anime* flashing against the
wall. The menu includes hot and cold appetizers, like asparagus
beef roll and spicy tuna salad.
(312) 491-9232, sushi-x.net, Mon–Fri 11–2, 5–11, Sat–Sun
5–11 ⊛

SWEET TAMARIND $$ / ★★
1034 W. Belmont (Kenmore), Lakeview
Thai
Owners lost their lease on Diversey, their original location for
almost 20 years, and relocated to this cute corner spot in 2008.
Named after a fruit juice used in Thai cooking, Sweet Tamarind
serves Northern Thai cuisine, like the Northern chicken curry
and walnut and raisin fried rice. (The owners also run Lemongrass, another BYOB, which serves an identical menu.)
(773) 281-5300, sweettamarindthaicuisine.com, Mon–Thurs
11–10, Fri–Sat 11–11, Sun 12–9 ⊛ ⚐

TA TONG $–$$ / ★★
2964 N. Lincoln (Wellington), Lakeview
Japanese/Thai
The owners of Ta Tong (the name is a combination of their nick-
names) gutted the interior of this space (formerly Café Demir),
added a sushi bar, and updated the decor with a contemporary,
Japanese-inspired touch. French doors in front offer a breezy spot
to dine on Thai noodle and rice dishes or a selection from the full
Japanese and maki menu. A large, unfinished back patio offers
additional seating in warmer months, and servers will stash your
bottles in a large cooler.
(773) 348-6500, Mon closed, Tues–Thurs 11:30–10, Fri–Sat
11:30–10:30, Sun 11:30–10 ⊛ ⚐

TABOUN GRILL $$$ / ★★
6339 N. California (Devon), West Rogers Park
Middle Eastern/Brunch

This family-oriented, kosher eatery is named for the traditional
clay oven used to bake their delicious pita bread. BYOB diners
must bring kosher wine (look for *mevushal* on the bottle), but any
type of beer or spirits is okay. Regulars rave about the kefta kebab
and *shawerma*, and on Sundays a Yeminite brunch menu is served
from 11–3.
(773) 381-2606, taboungrill.com, Sun–Thurs 11–10, Fri 11–2, Sat
closed (seasonal) ⊛

TABOUN GRILL $$$ / ★★
8808 Gross Point (Dempster), Skokie
Middle Eastern/Brunch

This sister location, which opened in 2009 in a small shopping
plaza, offers a menu that's identical to the West Rogers Park original. They also have the same BYOB policy (see previous listing).
(847) 965-1818, taboungrill.com, Sun–Thurs 11–10, Fri 11–2, Sat
closed (seasonal) ⊛

TAC QUICK THAI KITCHEN $ / ★★
3930 N. Sheridan (Dakin), Lakeview
Thai

There are myriad traditional Thai dishes to choose from at this
well-kept North Side secret. But the real fun begins when you ask
for the "secret" Thai menu, which offers more traditional, super-
spicy cuisine. Check out the *nam huang*, or Vietnamese-style pork
balls, served with rice papers, green apple, green banana, basil,
lettuce, and cucumber. To keep up with increasing demand, the
owner expanded into the space next door and remodeled with
relaxing earth tones.
(773) 327-5253, tacquick.com, Mon 11–10, Tues closed, Wed–Sat
11–10, Sun 11–9 ☂ ⚑

TAJ MAHAL $ / ★
1512 W. Taylor (Laflin), University Village/Little Italy
Indian/Pakistani
There are several ethnic BYOBs on this block of Taylor Street,
including this casual Indian spot. Owner Harish Gadapa offers
a full range of traditional Indian cuisine, including samosas,
tandoori chicken, vindaloo, curries, and nearly a dozen breads,
which are baked in-house. They'll chill your bottles in the fridge
and provide beer glasses and corkscrews on request.
(312) 226-6546, tajmahalfastfoods.com, 11–10 daily ⊛

TAKE ME OUT LET'S EAT CHINESE! $ / -
1502 W. 18th (Laflin), Pilsen
Pan-Asian
The specialty here is "Little Hotties," owner Karen Lim's modern
take on Korean chicken wings. Lim's wings are smothered in a
sauce that packs tons of heat (influenced by her father's recipe,
offered at his Albany Park eatery, Great Sea). Choose from other
Asian starters (egg rolls, crab Rangoon) and wok dishes (chop
suey, kung pao) to pair with your own bottle in the updated,
bright, 20-seat dining area. (And bring something sweet to
balance the heat.)
(312) 929-2509, takemeoutchinese.com, Mon–Sat 11–9:30, Sun
11–9 ⊛

TAMALES LO MEJOR DE GUERRERO $ / ★
7024 N. Clark (Lunt), Rogers Park
Mexican
This stretch of Clark Street offers a bevy of Latin eateries. As the
name suggests, this tiny BYOB is all about Guerrero, Mexico–
influenced tamales, or combinations of meat and veggies steamed
in blankets of fresh masa. Though the focus is on takeout service,
a few tables are available for a handful of diners.
(773) 338-6450, Mon closed, Tues–Sun 5a–8p ⊛

TAMALLI $ / ★★
2459 W. Armitage (Campbell), Logan Square
Mexican
Carlos Reyna, known for his other Logan Square eatery, Maiz,
cultivated this unique Mexican spot that is casual, cozy, and
several notches above a tamale stand. The specialty here is *tamal*,
or steamed corn or banana husk leaves filled with chorizo, *tinga,*
steak, or veggies. Wine glasses and corkscrews are available
upon request.
(773) 276-1441, Mon closed, Tues–Sun 5–10 ⚡

TANGO SUR $$$ / ★★
3763 N. Southport (Grace), Lakeview
Argentinian
This Argentinian steakhouse is well-known for three things:
its generous cuts of meat, the large sidewalk patio, and a
corkage-free BYOB policy. There are many other highlights, like
the *berenjena* (oven-baked eggplant with spinach, provolone,
parmesan, ricotta), homemade *chimichurri* sauce, empanadas,
and intimate candlelit atmosphere. Choose from several cuts of
beef, like filet mignon, bone-in rib eye, boneless strip, flap meat,
and short ribs. Though popular for dates, Tango Sur's shareable
entrées and festive atmosphere set the stage for large parties.
Jonesing for one of their empanadas? Pick one up at the grocery
store next door (same owners), which also sells Tango Sur's
famous *chimichurri* sauce.
(773) 477-5466, Mon–Thurs 5–10:30, Fri 5–11:30, Sat 3–11:30,
Sun 12–11, reservations recommended ♻ ⚑

TANK NOODLE $$ / ★★
4953–55 N. Broadway (Argyle), Uptown
Vietnamese
This noodle shop also goes by the name Pho Xe Tang, but in case
there's any confusion, just look for the jam-packed noodle shop
at the corner of Broadway and Argyle. Perhaps the most popular
Vietnamese joint on the block, Tank offers myriad noodle dishes,
congee (rice soup), and their house specialty, *pho*, beef noodle
soup with slices of beef, which comes with a side plate chock-full
of basil, limes, scallions, and bean sprouts.
(773) 878-2253, tanknoodle.com, Mon–Tues 8:30–10, Wed
closed, Thurs–Sat 8:30–10, Sun 8:30–9 ♻

TANOSHII $$$$ / ★★
5547 N. Clark (Gregory), Edgewater
Japanese
You can order straight from the menu here, but why would you?
Instead, give your list of likes and dislikes to owner "Sushi Mike"
or sidekick "Sushi Chris," who will then create customized,
made-to-order maki or sushi for you on the fly. The results are
photo-worthy, and the delicate balance of complex flavors and
textures used will make you wonder if this is, in fact, the first
time you've ever eaten sushi. It's artistry and improv and innova-
tive cuisine all at once—made with the highest quality of fish you
can find in Chicago.
(773) 878-6886, tanoshiichicago.com, Sun–Mon 4–10, Tues
closed, Wed–Thurs 4–11, Fri 4–12, Sat 2–12, reservations
recommended ◀

TASTE OF LEBANON $ / -
1509 W. Foster (Clark), Andersonville
Middle Eastern
This low-key takeout spot serves super-cheap falafel, *shawerma*,
kebabs, and other Middle Eastern chow. If Taste of Lebanon were
located elsewhere, it might not ever see a BYOB customer. But in
this gentrified neighborhood—complete with great wine stores—
it's now on the BYOB goers' radar.
(773) 334-1600, Mon–Sat 11–8, Sun closed ☺

TASTE OF PERU $$$ / ★★
6545 N. Clark (Arthur), Rogers Park
Peruvian
The focus at this lively, family-run joint is on the food and
festive atmosphere—not the decor or location. Highlights on the
seafood-based Peruvian menu are the paella, *papas rellenas*, and
lomo saltado, a rib eye sautéed with tomatoes, onions, and beer.
On weekends, expect a packed house and live Peruvian music.
Bring in a bottle of pisco and staff will mix up a batch of pisco
sours, a delicious lemony Peruvian drink.
(773) 381-4540, tasteofperu.com, Sun–Thurs 11:30–10, Fri–Sat
11:30–11 ◀ Ⓟ

TEENA MIA $ / ★
564 W. Washington (Jefferson), West Loop
Italian

Jerry Cerraro (Luigi's Beef, Asta La Pasta) is behind this busy breakfast and lunch spot, which attracts the West Loop business crowd and nearby residents. Not too many BYOB here since Teena Mia dropped its dinner menu, but it is welcome. The eggplant parmigiana and lasagna (the sausage is made in-house) are highly recommended.

(312) 441-9577, Mon–Fri 10:30–3:30, Sat–Sun closed ⊛

TERRAGUSTO $$$$ / ★★
1851 W. Addison (Wolcott), Lakeview
Italian

No doubt about it, this is some of the freshest Italian cuisine in town. Chef/owner Theo Gilbert strives for authentic trattoria-style dining, which involves four courses: antipasta, a pasta dish, a shared meat dish, and dessert (dishes can also be ordered à la carte). The pasta is made daily in-house, and seasonal ingredients are usually sourced locally. The menu rotates monthly, so check their Web site for current selections. Bistro-style glasses, wine chillers, and decanters are available.

(773) 248-2777, terragustocafe.com, Mon closed, Tues–Fri 6–10, Sat 5–10, Sun 5–9, reservations recommended ⌁

THAI AREE $ / ★★
3592 N. Milwaukee (Addison), Old Irving Park
Thai

In business since 1987, this neighborhood dinner spot offers a more authentic version of Thai. While staples like pad Thai remain favorites, the beef garlic (thinly sliced chargrilled beef, topped with garlic and sauce and served with fresh vegetables), peanut sauce noodle (wide noodles and choice of meat), and Thai sausages are mainstays on the menu. You may find Thai Aree closed during the second half of the summer, when the family takes its yearly vacation to Thailand ("our kitchen is way too hot in the summer, over 100 degrees, even with air conditioning," grumbles one family member).

(773) 725-6751, Mon–Sat 4–9, Sun closed ⊛

THAI AROMA $ / ★★
4142 N. Broadway (Buena), Uptown
Thai

The free parking lot makes this North Side place an easy choice
for lunch or dinner. The menu is similar to the one at Thai
Aroma's sister location in Old Town, except for the "Chef's
Favorite Entrées," which offer several more options, like the pad
Thai duck, spicy catfish, seafood curry, and Aroma pad Thai made
with glass noodles.
(773) 404-7777, aromachicago.com, 11–11 daily ⊛ Ⓟ

THAI AROMA $ / ★★
417 W. North (Sedgwick), Old Town
Thai

This sister location (a third location on Randolph Street closed)
offers a similar menu to its Uptown counterpart's. Wine glasses,
pint glasses, ice buckets, and corkscrews are available on request.
(312) 664-3400, aromachicago.com, Sun–Thurs 11–10, Fri–Sat
11–11 ⊛

THAI AVENUE $ / ★★
4949 N. Broadway (Argyle), Uptown
Thai

Although Thai Avenue's menu was originally designed to reflect
the food sold by street vendors in Thailand, it has evolved to a
more standard selection of Thai starters, salads, soups, noodle and
rice dishes, curries, and entrées. The banana egg roll appetizer—
deep-fried banana wrapped in a crispy shell, topped with honey
and sesame seeds—does double-duty as dessert.
(773) 878-2222, Mon closed, Tues–Thurs 11–9:30, Fri–Sat 11–10,
Sun 11–9 ⊛

THAI BINH $$ / ★★
1113 W. Argyle (Winthrop), Uptown
Vietnamese
The Vietnamese culture is very family-oriented, and children are
often seen running around the casual eateries in this area or, in
Thai Binh's case, taking on hostess duties and busing tables. The
family-friendly approach continues to the way food is served, on
shareable lazy Susans in the middle of each table, where folks
indulge in traditional Vietnamese noodle soups, rice dishes, and
more. They provide wine glasses and ice buckets and will put
your bottles in the cooler on request.
(773) 728-0283, 11–11 daily ✆

THAI BOWL $ / -
1049 W. Taylor (Carpenter), University Village/Little Italy
Thai
This cozy eatery focuses on takeout and delivery service to the
regular stream of students in the neighborhood. But in warmer
months, there's a large outdoor courtyard/garden where diners
can slurp down one of Thai Bowl's fresh smoothies or feast on
a bowl of noodles. Good luck finding wine or beer glasses or a
corkscrew, though; at this place, you better bring your own.
(312) 226-9129, thaibowlnoodle.com, 11–10 daily ✆ 🌱

THAI CLASSIC $ / ★★
3332 N. Clark (Buckingham), Lakeview
Thai
Not much has changed at this Lakeview mainstay since it opened
in 1989, and that's precisely the reason for its charm (not that it's
a hole-in-the-wall or in need of remodeling). Thai Classic offers a
more authentic Thai dining experience, with a few sunken tables
(remove your shoes at the door) and a menu that veers off the
beaten path of other Thai eateries in the area. For something different, try the potato curry puffs, duck bamboo, spicy drunken fried
rice, orchid chicken, catfish *pad ped,* or one of the daily specials.
(773) 404-2000, thaiclassicrestaurant.com, 11:30–10 daily ✆

THAI EATERY $ / ★★
2234 N. Western (Lyndale), Bucktown
Thai
In this case, good things do come in small packages. Thai Eatery's
tiny kitchen serves savory Thai dishes that lean toward more
authentic cuisine in a tight, 24-seat space. Find mouthwatering
gang moo tapo (spinach and pork in tamarind curry and coconut
milk) and tomato beef over rice, onions, and peppers alongside
standards like tom yum soup and pad Thai.
(773) 394-3035, Mon closed, Tues–Sun 11:30–10 ⊛

THAI 55 $ / ★★
1607 E. 55th (Cornell), Hyde Park
Thai
According to the owners, this is the oldest Thai restaurant in
Hyde Park. One thing's for certain: They have one of the most
extensive menus of any Thai restaurant in the area. In addition
to the standard Thai dishes, Thai 55 offers several items from its
off-the-beaten-path "deluxe menu" and about 20 stir-fry options.
(773) 363-7119, thai55restaurant.com, 11–10 daily ⊛

THAI GRILL $ / ★★
1040 W. Granville (Kenmore), Edgewater
Thai
Located on the ground floor of the former Sovereign Hotel (now a
high-rise apartment building), Thai Grill offers a charming, casual
space to feast on Thai favorites such as massaman curry (vegetarian curry stew of tofu, potatoes, mixed vegetables, coconut milk,
and peanuts) and combination meals (entrée or noodle dishes
plus an appetizer), which are available nightly for less than $10. A
private party room on the side accommodates up to 50 people for
a budget-friendly BYOB party.
(773) 274-7510, thaigrillchicago.com, Mon closed, Tues–Sun
11:30–10 ⊛ ♥ Ⓟ

THAI LAGOON $ / ★
2322 W. North (Claremont), Bucktown
Pan-Asian

With two bars, this west Bucktown eatery is certainly set up for a liquor license, but they've been operating as a BYOB since opening in 1996. The menu is mostly Thai, punctuated with a few bursts of Vietnamese, Chinese, and Japanese. A reasonably priced selection of sushi and maki is served on Fridays and Saturdays. (773) 489-5747, thai-lagoon.com, Sun–Thurs 5–10, Fri–Sat 5–11 🦐

THAI LINDA CAFÉ $ / ★★
2022 W. Roscoe (Damen), Roscoe Village
Thai

Surprisingly, Thai Linda Café is the only BYOB on this strip of independently owned boutiques, restaurants, wine shops, and bars (as of press time). Owner Linda's husband Charley owns another BYOB, Charley Thai (in Logan Square), which offers an identical menu that leans toward traditional, not contemporary, Thai. Wine glasses, ice buckets, and corkscrews are available on request. (773) 868-0075, lindacharleythai.com, Sun–Thurs 4–10, Fri–Sat 11–10:30 🐝 🌂

THAI ON CLARK $ / ★★
4641 N. Clark (Wilson), Ravenswood
Thai

Unlike most neighborhood Thai joints, where pad Thai seems to be the most ordered dish, Thai On Clark's curries (yellow, green, red, panang) are the most popular items on the menu. Owners use a complex mix of spices for a more authentic taste, evident not only in their curries but in starters like tom yum soup. (773) 275-2620, Mon–Thurs 11–9:30, Fri–Sat 11–10, Sun closed 🐝

THAI OSCAR $$ / ★★
4638 N. Western (Eastwood), Lincoln Square
Japanese/Thai

New owner Pannika Sakulsorn recently took over this long-standing neighborhood place, which used to feature about 500 menu items (complete with photos). Though whittled down, Thai Oscar's menu still offers a wide range of what Sakulsorn describes as "American" and "real" Thai dishes, and an especially impressive maki selection.

(773) 878-5922, thaioscarrestaurant.com, Mon 11–10, Tues closed, Wed–Thurs 11–10, Fri–Sat 11–11, Sun 4–10 ⊛

THAI PASTRY $ / ★★
4925 N. Broadway (Ainslie), Uptown
Thai

Aumphai Kusab's quaint pastry-shop-turned-restaurant made a huge media splash a few years ago, but the buzz seems to have died down somewhat, making it a little easier to get a table here (except on the weekends). They provide basic beverage service, but keep in mind that underage servers can't legally touch your booze.

(773) 784-5399, thaipastry.com, Sun–Thurs 11–10, Fri–Sat 11–11, reservations recommended on weekends ⊛

THAI PASTRY 2 $ / ★★
7350 W. Lawrence (Oketo), Harwood Heights
Thai

This 50-seat sister location serves an identical menu (though not as wide of a pastry selection).

(708) 867-8840, 11–10 daily ⊛ Ⓟ

THAI SMILE $ / ★★
12241 S. Harlem (123rd), Palos Heights
Thai

I found my first encounter with host "Me" and his innocuously straightforward communication style charming at this casual, 40-seat Thai spot. But what the place lacks in gloss or sophistication it makes up for with fresh, made-to-order Thai. One tip: Be just as straightforward when telling the staff how you like your food, i.e., level of spice, vegetarian, etc. It's just how they roll.

(708) 448-9888, Mon closed, Tues–Sat 11:30–9:30, Sun 4–9 ⊛ Ⓟ

THAI SPICE $$$ / ★★
1320 W. Devon (Wayne), Rogers Park
Japanese/Thai

Yes, you read the average entrée price correctly in this listing.
While some of the rice and noodle dishes are slightly cheaper,
even curries are about $14.95, and the portions are not necessar-
ily family-sized. The confusion does not end there: A smattering
of maki rolls was introduced to the menu recently, nearly identical
to those found at Sushi X (the owner trained with their sushi
chefs, but why not create his own?).
(773) 973-0504, Mon closed, Tues–Thurs 4–10, Fri–Sat 4–11,
Sun 4–10 ⊛

THAI THANK YOU $ / ★★
3248 N. Lincoln (Belmont), Lakeview
Thai

Like so many other restaurants, Thai Thank You opened as a
BYOB to attract bargain hunters during the recession. There's a
built-in bar waiting for the day when things turn around, but
for right now, enjoy the savings. Owners updated the decor with
leather banquettes and a palette of relaxing earth tones. The menu
is standard Thai, save for the Thai classic omelette and house
specialties (thank you noodles and thank you fried rice). Wine
glasses, ice buckets, and corkscrews are available on request.
(773) 348-7199, thaithankyou.com, 11–10 daily ⊛

THAI UPTOWN $ / ★★
4621 N. Broadway (Wilson), Uptown
Thai

Many claim "authentic" Thai cuisine, but this unpretentious place
delivers. Highlights include the Thai Uptown special—a mix of
chicken or shrimp stir-fried with tom yum sauce, onion, tomato,
and mushroom—and the delectable coconut ice cream, which is
made in-house.
(773) 561-9999, thaiuptown.com, Mon–Sat 11:30–9:30, Sun
closed ⊛

THAI VALLEY $ / -
4600 N. Kedzie (Wilson), Albany Park
Thai
Located on a row of mostly Middle Eastern eateries, this long-
standing neighborhood spot is suitable for a business lunch
or casual dinner. A few unique items, like the *nue numtok*
(charbroiled beef, onions, roasted rice, sour spicy sauce) and *gang
mhotapo* (spinach and pork in tamarind curry and coconut milk)
punctuate the otherwise standard Thai menu. Bring your own
corkscrew and stemware.
(773) 588-2020, Mon closed, Tues–Sun 11:30–10 ⊛

THAI VILLAGE $ / ★★
2053 W. Division (Hoyne), Wicker Park
Thai
This reliable Thai spot has been serving the Wicker Park neighborhood for over a decade. Though the menu is a predictable
selection of Thai standards, every dish is well-seasoned, fresh,
and made-to-order. The dining room, a dimly lit space filled with
Thai artifacts and dark woods, is in contrast to the sun-drenched
sidewalk patio, a great people-watching place to enjoy generous
helpings of pad Thai or *pad se ewe* with a glass of wine (unless the
city says otherwise) in the summer.
(773) 384-5352, 11:30–10 daily ⊛ ⋈

35TH STREET CAFÉ $ / ★★
1735 W. 35th (Hermitage), McKinley Park
Eclectic
Chef/co-owner Enrique Gutierrez has been all over the culinary
map, literally and figuratively. He brings his vast experiences,
which range from stints in Egypt and Spain to Hard Rock Cafe
and The Cheesecake Factory, to this 65-seat eatery with a menu
that hopscotches from Chinese to Italian to Mexican.
(773) 523-3500, 35thstreetcafe.com, Mon–Fri 7–8, Sat 7–6, Sun
7–4 ⊛ ⋈ �

TOMATO HEAD $ / -
945 W. Randolph (Morgan), West Loop
Italian
BYOB was forbidden at this string of pizza joints until new owners took over in 2008. Now, customers are welcome to bring their
own beer or wine to any of the locations. Tomato Head's thin-
crust 'za is handmade and topped with creative combinations like
the fire breather (pepperoni and hot peppers) and Zorbazah (feta
cheese, kalamata olives, tomatoes). Bring your own corkscrews
and glasses; there's no beverage service.
(312) 226-1616, gettomatohead.com, Sun–Thurs 11–11, Fri–Sat
11–1 ⊛

TOMATO HEAD $ / -
823 W. Eastman (Halsted), Lincoln Park
Italian
(312) 642-6700, gettomatohead.com, Mon–Sat 11–10, Sun
11–9 ⊛

TOMATO HEAD $ / -
1162 Wilmette (Central), Wilmette
Italian
(847) 853-0055, gettomatohead.com, Mon–Thurs 4–9, Fri–Sat
11–10, Sun 11–9 ⊛

TORO SUSHI $$$$ / ★★★
2546 N. Clark (Wrightwood), Lincoln Park
Japanese
Mitch Kim polished his sushi skills at Nikko in Arlington Heights
and Sushi O Sushi in Chicago before opening this much-revered
spot in 2005. Kim has received tons of positive press for his
high-quality, specialty maki rolls and sushi, and he serves only
the freshest of fish. There are also a few items available from the
kitchen, but why bother when the sushi's this good? Wine glasses,
sake cups, ice buckets, and corkscrews are available on request.
(773) 348-4877, Mon closed, Tues–Thurs 5–9:30, Fri–Sat 12–2,
5–10, Sun 4–9 ⊛

TRATTORIA CATERINA $$ / ★★
616 S. Dearborn (Harrison), South Loop
Italian

Trattoria Caterina continues to keep pace with the growing
neighborhood; they expanded into the office space next door,
thereby doubling their size. Sticking to what works, they haven't
modified their menu, an extensive variety of traditional Northern
and Southern Italian cuisine served in a white-linen tablecloth,
yet friendly neighborhood, setting.

(312) 939-7606, Mon–Thurs 11–9, Fri 11–10, Sat 8–9, Sun
8–noon, reservations recommended on weekends ⊛ ⋒

TRE KRONOR $$$ / ★★★
3258 W. Foster (Sawyer), Albany Park
Scandinavian/Brunch

Since 1992, regulars have been flocking to this charming, bistro-
style eatery for breakfast, lunch, dinner, and weekend brunch.
The kitchen is experimenting with some contemporary items on
the dinner menu, like roasted chicken with tarragon and juniper
berries, and crab cakes with roasted red pepper sauce. Sidewalk
and back patio seating areas offer optimal people-watching spots.
There are plenty of Champagne flutes on hand, so bring some
bubbly and mix up some mimosas at weekend brunch.

(773) 267-9888, trekronorrestaurant.com, Mon–Sat 7–10, Sun
9–3, reservations recommended (not taken for weekend brunch)
⊛ ⋒

TREAT $$$ / ★★
1616 N. Kedzie (North), Humboldt Park
Eclectic/Brunch

Now that Treat has been featured on *Check, Please!* the word is out
about this quirky BYOB. The atmosphere is unpretentious and
comfortable at this 32-seat place, where local art is displayed on
the walls and a diner-style counter serves as additional seating in
front. But don't let the casual vibe fool you: The Indian-influenced
menu caters to gourmet tastes, especially the calamari with aioli,
curried gnocchi, and masala French toast (served for weekend
brunch). They provide wine glasses, corkscrews, and ice buckets
on request.

(773) 772-1201, treatrestaurant.com, Mon–Fri 5–10, Sat–Sun
9–10 ⋌ ⋒

T-SPOT SUSHI & TEA BAR $$$ / ★★
3925 N. Lincoln (Larchmont), North Center
Japanese

This beautifully decorated, cozy place offers a more unique approach to sushi. Rather than the usual, mile-long selection of specialty maki rolls, the menu focuses on inventive flavor combinations and a small, more classic selection of sushi, sashimi, and maki. There's a daily happy hour menu from 5–6 and daily entrée specials for $14.95. Of course, the owners would prefer you sip a cup or pot of one of their many loose teas, but BYOB is allowed.
(773) 549-4500, tspotsushiandteabar.com, Mon–Thurs 5–10, Fri 5–11, Sat 12–11, Sun closed, reservations recommended on weekends ⊛ 🐟

TULUM GRILL $ / ★★
1800 W. Grand (Wood), West Town
American/Mexican/Brunch

New owners took over LT's (Larry Tucker's old place) and redecorated with contemporary Mexican colors. The size of this storefront eatery—80 seats plus counter space—is deceiving from the outside. Chef/owner Ricardo Romo serves up eggs about 20 different ways for breakfast and Mexican/American sandwiches, wraps, and salads for lunch. Plans for a dinner menu are in the works.
(312) 997-2400, 8–3 daily ⊛

TURKISH CUISINE & BAKERY $$ / ★★★
5605 N. Clark (Bryn Mawr), Edgewater
Turkish

Choose from 76 (numbered on the menu for convenience) choices for seafood, desserts made in-house, and traditional Georgian dishes such as the moussaka-like *karniyarik* and *tokat kebab* (juicy lamb). Also delish are the Turkish *pide*, or oven-baked pies stuffed with feta cheese, beef, eggs, or veggies. Belly dancers liven up the joint on weekends.
(773) 878-8930, turkishcuisine.net, Mon–Thurs 11–11, Fri–Sat 11–12, Sun 5–10, reservations recommended on weekends ⊛

UDUPI PALACE $$ / ★★
2543 W. Devon (Rockwell), West Rogers Park
Indian/Vegetarian
This is one of the few places on Devon to offer made-to-order
Southern Indian cuisine (read: vegetarian). Their charming dining
room is a few notches above other eateries in the area. Another
highlight? The wide variety of traditional *dosai*, or crepes. Basic
beverage service is provided on request.
(773) 338-2152, udupipalace.com, 11:30–10 daily, reservations
recommended on weekends ⊛

UMAIYA CAFÉ $ / ★★
1605 W. Montrose (Ashland), Ravenswood
Pan-Asian
More and more places around town offer sushi alongside Thai
food or other Asian fare. Umaiya ("delicious" in Japanese) joins
the pack, but offers a few fusion dishes (Thailand maki, teriyaki
noodle) for an original twist. With just one bathroom, this casual
takeout spot is not likely to get a liquor license anytime soon.
(773) 404-1109, umaiya.com, Mon–Wed 11:30–10, Thurs closed,
Fri–Sat 11:30–10, Sun 4–10 ⊛

UNCLE JOE'S $$ / ★
8211 S. Cottage Grove (E. 82nd), South Side
Caribbean
Jamaican native Joe Neish is behind this string of Caribbean
joints, famous for jerk chicken and the vinegar-based "Uncle
Joe's Jerk Sauce" (sold on-site and at local grocery stores). Neish
prepares his own rubs for jerk chicken, seafood, and other cuts
of meat (oxtail, goat), which come with rice, peas, and plantains.
This original site seats 40 (two others, not listed in this book,
only offer carryout, not dine-in, service).
(773) 962-9935, unclejoesjerk.com, Mon–Thurs 11–10, Fri–Sat
1–11, Sun 1–10 ⊛

UNCLE JOE'S $$ / ★
4655 S. King Drive (E. 47th), South Side
Caribbean
This is the largest Uncle Joe's location, with 180 seats. They may be getting a liquor license sometime in 2010–2011, so call ahead to make sure they're still BYOB.
(773) 962-9935, unclejoesjerk.com, Mon–Thurs 11–10, Fri–Sat 11–11, Sun 1–10 ⊛

UNCLE JOE'S $$ / ★
1461 E. Hyde Park Blvd. (Blackstone), Hyde Park
Caribbean
(773) 241-5550, unclejoesjerk.com, Mon–Thurs 11–10, Fri–Sat 11–11, Sun 12–9 ⊛

UNCLE'S KABAB $ / -
2816 W. Devon (California), West Rogers Park
Middle Eastern
This family-friendly, neighborhood place serves Middle Eastern classics (kebabs, lentil soup, hummus) in a diner-like atmosphere to a mostly Muslim customer base (owners claim that all the meat served here is halal, which is a designation similar to kosher). For something off the beaten path, try the *borak*, a fried turnover filled with ground beef, or the potato chop sandwich.
(773) 338-3134, 10:30–10 daily ⊛

URBAN BELLY $$ / ★
3053 N. California (Nelson), Logan Square
Pan-Asian
Bill Kim (Le Lan, Charlie Trotter's) and wife Yvonne Cadiz-Kim took a detour from their fine-dining backgrounds for this fast-casual noodle shop. But even the out-of-the-way location, communal tables, cafeteria-style dining, and minimal beverage service (bistro glasses and corkscrews only) haven't stopped foodies and wine connoisseurs from crowding this gem. One dip into the masterfully flavored broths (soba with bay scallops, udon with shrimp) and dumplings (chicken and mushroom, lamb and brandy), and you'll have no problem understanding why.
(773) 583-0500, urbanbellychicago.com, Mon closed, Tues–Sun 11–9 ⊛

URU-SWATI $ / ★★
2629 W. Devon (Talman), West Rogers Park
Indian/Vegetarian
Uru-Swati ("morning star of peace") is a haven for health-
conscious diners in search of authentic Indian cuisine. Though
this small spot has only 14 tables, the menu is an exhaustive
selection of vegetarian "quick bites" (rice pancakes, fried lentil
donuts, samosas, puffed rice with chutney) that reflect the
street-snack style of food common throughout India. Dinner
entrées (*chana masala, malai kofta*) are also available.
(773) 262-5280, uru-swati.net, Sun–Tues 11–9, Wed closed, Thurs
11–9, Fri–Sat 11–10 🥬

VILLA ROSA $$ / ★
5345 W. Devon (Minnehaha), Northwest Side
Italian
This family-run pizza joint also serves a large variety of pasta,
ribs, chicken, sides, salads, and a few Mexican eats. Everything
is made-to-order with fresh ingredients, from the chicken pesto
mostaccioli to the slabs of BBQ ribs. They provide plastic cups
and corkscrews. No hard alcohol allowed.
(773) 774-7107, Sun–Thurs 11–9, Fri–Sat 11–10 🥬

WHOLLY FRIJOLES $$ / ★★
3908 W. Touhy (Crawford), Lincolnwood
Mexican
Chef/co-owner Carmen Villegas runs this popular BYOB, which
offers contemporary gourmet Mexican cuisine. Villegas opened
this restaurant in 2000, after working for Lettuce Entertain You
and Pump Room, to offer updated twists on classics, like gazpa-
cho salad and braised leg of lamb in chipotle sauce. The rotating
specials run from masa boats with lobster and poblano peppers
to banana and coconut ice cream. This place is always packed,
and they don't take reservations, but you can call ahead and place
your name on a waiting list.
(847) 329-9810, whollyfrijolesgrill.com, Mon–Thurs 11–9, Fri
11–9:30, Sat 11–10, Sun closed 🥬 🌿 Ⓟ

WINGS O' FLAVOR $ / -
3109 N. Halsted (Briar), Lakeview
Eclectic

This carryout joint specializes in jumbo-sized party wings. Choose from Jamaican jerk, Chicago-style honey BBQ, Louisiana Cajun, Thai sweet chili, New York buffalo, Texas chipotle, and Caribbean lemon pepper. Though most people take their order to go, there are about 16 seats and a flat-screen TV, which always has a game on. Free parking in the CVS parking lot next door.
(773) 697-7032, Mon 2:30–10:30, Tues–Thurs 11:30–10:30, Fri–Sat 11:30–12:30, Sun closed (open during football season)
🐣 Ⓟ

YASSA $$ / ★★★
716 E. 79th (Cottage Grove), South Side
African

This Chatham neighborhood gem has received a lot of local ink for its slow-cooked, Senegalese food. Husband-wife team Madieye and Awa Gueye graciously serve generous portions of African classics like yassa chicken or fish (marinated in lemon, onions, and mustard), *dibi* (lamb chops crusted with black pepper, cumin, and clove) and *maffe* (lamb stew with peanut butter and yams).
(773) 488-5599, yassaafricanrestaurant.com, Sun–Thurs 11–10, Fri–Sat 11–11 🐣 Ⓟ

YES THAI $ / ★★★
5211 N. Damen (Foster), Lincoln Square
Thai

Hands down, this is one of the best neighborhood Thai restaurants in the city. The crab Rangoon is second-to-none, the noodles are always prepared perfectly (never tangled in a mushy mess), the veggies crisp and fresh, and each dish is well-seasoned with balanced flavors. They provide Champagne buckets, red and white wine glasses, and corkscrews on request.
(773) 878-3487, yesthaichicago.com, Mon–Thurs 11:30–9:30, Fri–Sat 11:30–10:30, Sun 3–9, reservations recommended on weekends 🐣 🏴

YOLK $ / ★
1120 S. Michigan (11th), South Loop
Eclectic/Brunch
There's something for everyone at this unique, contemporary
breakfast and lunch spot, from hearty skillets and frittatas to
French toast and oatmeal (served three ways). Yolk's freshly
squeezed juices (strawberry/orange, grapefruit, tomato, others)
lend themselves to mimosas or fruity cocktails (but bring your
own stemware if necessary; they only have juice glasses). Validated parking is available at either location for $2.
(312) 789-9655, yolk-online.com, Mon–Fri 6–3, Sat–Sun 7–3 ⊛

YOLK $ / ★
747 N. Wells (Chicago), River North
Eclectic/Brunch
(312) 787-2277, yolk-online.com, Mon–Fri 6–3, Sat–Sun 7–3 ⊛

YUM THAI $ / ★
7748 W. Madison (Park), Forest Park
Thai
A reliable neighborhood place, Yum Thai offers a standard variety
of Thai classics. Though they focus on carryout and delivery
service, there is a 24-seat dining room to enjoy a casual BYOB
meal. Beverage service can be spotty, so you may want to bring
your own bottle opener just in case.
(708) 366-8888, Mon closed, Tues–Thurs 11:30–9, Fri–Sat 11:30–
10, Sun 4–9 ⊛ Ⓟ

YUMMY THAI $ / ★★
1418 W. Taylor (Loomis), University Village/Little Italy
Thai
Though a tad corny, the name of this place is fitting—yummy
smells emanate from the flaming woks in the kitchen. Students
and neighborhood regulars stream into this above-average Thai
spot, which caters to dine-in as well as delivery and takeout
customers. Nothing too unusual about the menu (standard Thai
apps, soups, noodle and rice dishes, curries), except for a handful
of Chinese and Japanese items.
(312) 633-0003, yummythaichicago.com, Mon–Fri 11–9, Sat–Sun
12–9 ⊛

YUMMY YUMMY $ / ★★
2901 N. Broadway (Oakdale), Lakeview
Pan-Asian
For such a tiny place, Yummy Yummy's kitchen cranks out an
impressive variety of dishes from all over Asia. The menu is predominantly Chinese, but a few Thai, Japanese, and Korean dishes
pop up, especially among the appetizers and noodle dishes. They
also offer over 50 vegetarian appetizers, soups, and entrées for
lunch and dinner.
(773) 525-6677, 12–10:30 daily ⊛

ZAPP $ / ★★
2927 W. Devon (Richmond), West Rogers Park
Thai
This is the newest Thai restaurant from the same family behind
Siam Pasta, Spoon Thai, and Mama Thai, to name a few. Due to
the high Muslim population in the area, most of Zapp's customers
don't drink; therefore, there aren't plans to apply for a liquor
license anytime soon. So enjoy your own bottle of Riesling in the
meantime. Karaoke fans can belt out Bon Jovi until the wee hours
Fridays thru Sundays.
(773) 743-0297, Mon–Thurs 11–10, Fri–Sat 11–11, Sun
12–10 ⊛

ZOBA THE NOODLE SHOP $$ / ★
1565 Sherman (Davis), Evanston
Pan-Asian
Yaki soba, udon, pad Thai, kung pao, and other made-from-
scratch noodles dishes dominate the menu at this casual, cheery
spot, popular with the Northwestern University crowd. They
provide water glasses, corkscrews, and ice buckets on request.
(847) 328-9622, zobanoodlebar.com, Mon–Thurs 11–9:30,
Fri–Sat 11–10, Sun 12–9 ⊛

Restaurants That Allow BYOB for Corkage Fees of $0–$50*

Although the following restaurants have a fully stocked bar or comprehensive wine list, they allow customers to BYOB for a corkage fee ranging from zilch to a whopping $50. While not exhaustive, this list does represent a wide variety of city and suburban locations, price points, cuisines, and corkage fees. Before you go, here's a quick refresher on etiquette when bringing your own bottle to a restaurant with a liquor license:

- Order a second bottle of wine or a round of drinks from the restaurant.

- It's always a good idea to call ahead both to let the staff know what bottle you are bringing and to confirm the corkage fee and what type of glassware they have.

- Tip on service. If in doubt as to how much, double or triple the wine's retail price and tip on this amount. Or, tip on the average price of a bottle on the restaurant's list.

- Limit to one or two bottles per table.

- Do not bring a wine on the restaurant's list.

- Make sure the restaurant has the proper equipment (decanters, etc.).

- Offer a taste to the chef or sommelier.

- Can't finish your bottle? Ask for a resealable plastic bag to go, per Illinois' amended open container law.

*Corkage fees were current as of press time.

A TAVOLA
2148 W. Chicago (Leavitt), Ukrainian Village, (773) 276-7567
Italian
Corkage: $20

ADOBO GRILL
1610 N. Wells (North), Old Town, (773) 252-9990
Nuevo Latino
Corkage: $15, waived if the vintage is more than 10 years old

AGAMI
4712 N. Broadway (Leland), Uptown, (773) 506-1854
Japanese
Corkage: $30; none on Mondays

AI
358 W. Ontario (Orleans), River North, (312) 335-9888
Japanese
Corkage: $20

AMARIND'S
6822 W. North (Oak Park Ave.), Elmwood Park, (773) 889-9999
Thai
Corkage: $7 for wine, $1.50 per 16-oz. beer

AMARIT
600 S. Dearborn (Harrison), South Loop, (312) 939-1179
Thai
Corkage: none; beer and wine allowed

ANTEPRIMA
5316 N. Clark (Berwyn), Andersonville, (773) 506-9990
Italian
Corkage: $20

ARYA BHAVAN
2508 W. Devon (Campbell), West Rogers Park, (773) 274-5800
Indian/Vegetarian
Corkage: $3 per person

Corkage fees are per 750 mL bottle of wine. Only BYO wines to these
restaurants (unless beer, spirits, or sake is indicated). Do not bring a wine
on the restaurant's list.

AVENUES
108 E. Superior (Rush), Gold Coast, (312) 573-6754
French
Corkage: $38; none on Tuesdays

BARRINGTON COUNTRY BISTRO
700 W. Northwest Hwy. (Hart), Barrington, (847) 842-1300
French
Corkage: $20

BEN PAO
52 W. Illinois (Michigan), Gold Coast, (312) 222-1888
Chinese
Corkage: $15

BICE
158 E. Ontario (Michigan), Gold Coast, (312) 664-1474
Italian
Corkage: $20

BISTRO CAMPAGNE
4518 N. Lincoln (Sunnyside), Lincoln Square, (773) 271-6100
French
Corkage: $15

BISTRO MARGOT
1437 N. Wells (Schiller), Old Town, (312) 587-3660
French
Corkage: $15

BISTRO 110
110 E. Pearson (Rush), Gold Coast, (312) 266-3110
French
Corkage: $15

BISTRO ZINC
1131 N. State (Elm), Gold Coast, (312) 337-1131
French
Corkage: $25

BLACKBIRD
619 W. Randolph (Des Plaines), West Loop, (312) 715-0708
Eclectic
Corkage: $25; two-bottle limit

BLUE FIN
1952 W. North (Damen), Wicker Park, (773) 394-7373
Japanese
Corkage: none for 1–7 people; $3.50 per person thereafter

BLUE NILE
6118 N. Ravenswood (Peterson), West Rogers Park,
(773) 465-6710
Ethiopian
Corkage: $2.50 per person

BOB CHINN'S CRAB HOUSE
393 S. Milwaukee (Dundee), Wheeling, (847) 520-3633
Seafood
Corkage: $10

BOKA
1729 N. Halsted (Willow), Lincoln Park, (773) 337-6070
Contemporary American
Corkage: $25, waived if the vintage is more than 25 years old

BRANMOR'S AMERICAN GRILL
300 S. Veterans Pkwy. (Lily Cache Lane), Bolingbrook,
(630) 226-9926
American
Corkage: $15

BUONA TERRA
2535 N. California (Logan Blvd.), Logan Square, (773) 289-3800
Italian
Corkage: $15

Corkage fees are per 750 mL bottle of wine. Only BYO wines to these
restaurants (unless beer, spirits, or sake is indicated). Do not bring a wine
on the restaurant's list.

CAFÉ LUCCI
609 Milwaukee (Central), Glenview, (847) 729-2268
Italian
Corkage: $20

CAFÉ MATOU
1846 N. Milwaukee (Moffat), Bucktown, (773) 384-8911
French
Corkage: $10

CAFÉ 28
1800 W. Irving Park (Ravenswood), North Center,
(773) 528-2883
Nuevo Latino
Corkage: $10

CARLOS'
429 Temple (Waukegan), Highland Park, (847) 432-0770
French
Corkage: $30; none on Mondays and Fridays

CHALKBOARD
4343 N. Lincoln (Montrose), North Center, (773) 477-7144
Contemporary American
Corkage: $15

CHEF'S STATION
915 Davis (Maple), Evanston, (847) 570-9821
Contemporary American
Corkage: $15

CHICAGO CHOP HOUSE
60 W. Ontario (State), Near North, (312) 787-7100
Steakhouse
Corkage: $25

CHIYO
3800 W. Lawrence (Hamlin), Albany Park, (773) 267-1555
Japanese
Corkage: $15

COCO
2723 W. Division (California), Humboldt Park, (773) 384-4811
Puerto Rican
Corkage: $15

COURTRIGHT'S
8989 Archer, Willow Springs, (708) 839-8000
French
Corkage: $20

D & J BISTRO
466 S. Rand (Main), Lake Zurich, (847) 438-8001
French
Corkage: $15

DAVE'S ITALIAN KITCHEN
1635 Chicago (Church), Evanston, (847) 475-6044
Italian
Corkage: $8

DAVIS ST. FISHMARKET
501 Davis (Hinman), Evanston, (847) 869-3474
Seafood
Corkage: $15

DINOTTO
215 W. North (Wells), Old Town, (312) 202-0302
Italian
Corkage: $15

DOZIKA
601 Dempster (Chicago), Evanston, (847) 869-9740
Pan-Asian
Corkage: $15 for wine, $3 per 16-oz. beer

ERWIN
2925 N. Halsted (Oakdale), Lakeview, (773) 528-7200
Contemporary American
Corkage: $20

Corkage fees are per 750 mL bottle of wine. Only BYO wines to these restaurants (unless beer, spirits, or sake is indicated). Do not bring a wine on the restaurant's list.

ETHIOPIAN DIAMOND
6120 N. Broadway (Granville), Edgewater, (773) 338-6100
Ethiopian
Corkage: $5

EVERGREEN RESTAURANT
2411 S. Wentworth (24th), Chinatown, (312) 225-8898
Chinese
Corkage: $5

FEAST
1616 N. Damen (North), Bucktown, (773) 772-7100
Eclectic
Corkage: $10; none on Mondays and Tuesdays

FEAST
25 E. Delaware (State), Gold Coast, (312) 337-4001
Eclectic
Corkage: $25

FIDDLEHEAD CAFÉ
4600 N. Lincoln (Wilson), Lincoln Square, (773) 751-1500
Eclectic
Corkage: $15

FOLLIA
953 W. Fulton (Morgan), West Loop, (312) 243-2888
Italian
Corkage: $25; wine must be Italian

FONDA DEL MAR
3749 W. Fullerton (Hamlin), Logan Square, (773) 489-3748
Nuevo Latino
Corkage: $15

FORNELLO TRATTORIA
1011 W. Irving Park (Sheridan), Lakeview, (773) 404-2210
Italian
Corkage: $9.95

FRIED GREEN TOMATOES
213 N. Main St. (Perry), Galena, (815) 777-3938
Italian
Corkage: $10

FRIENDSHIP RESTAURANT
2830 N. Milwaukee (Diversey), Logan Square, (773) 227-0970
Chinese
Corkage: $8

FRONTERA GRILL
445 N. Clark (Illinois), Near North, (312) 661-1434
Mexican
Corkage: $25

GABRIEL'S
310 Green Bay Rd. (Highwood Ave.), Highwood, (847) 433-0031
French/Italian
Corkage: $50

GAETANO'S
7636 W. Madison (Des Plaines), Forest Park, (708) 366-4010
Italian
Corkage: $18

GALE STREET INN
4914 N. Milwaukee (Higgins), Northwest Side, (773) 725-1300
American
Corkage: $10

GEJA'S CAFÉ
340 W. Armitage (Orleans), Lincoln Park, (773) 281-9101
Fondue
Corkage: $15; if bottle is purchased at The Poison Cup, Geja's will
waive the corkage fee or credit $25 toward the purchase of two
premier dinners

Corkage fees are per 750 mL bottle of wine. Only BYO wines to these
restaurants (unless beer, spirits, or sake is indicated). Do not bring a wine
on the restaurant's list.

GENE & GEORGETTI
500 N. Franklin (Illinois), River North, (312) 527-3718
Italian
Corkage: $25

GIO
1631 Chicago (Davis), Evanston, (847) 869-3900
Italian
Corkage: $15

GIOCO
1312 S. Wabash (13th), South Loop, (312) 939-3870
Italian
Corkage: $25

GLENN'S DINER
1820 W. Montrose (Wolcott), Ravenswood, (773) 506-1720
Seafood
Corkage: $5 for wine or six-pack of beer

GRAHAM ELLIOT
217 W. Huron (Franklin), River North, (312) 624-9975
Contemporary American
Corkage: $25

GREEK ISLANDS
200 S. Halsted (Adams), Greek Town, (312) 782-9855
Greek
Corkage: $15 for wine, $20 for Champagne

HAI YEN
1055 W. Argyle (Winthrop), Uptown, (773) 561-4077
Vietnamese
Corkage: $6

HIMAWARI
166 W. Wing (Vail), Arlington Heights, (847) 671-1601
Japanese
Corkage: $10, waived if wine is purchased at Tuscan Market

JANE'S
1655 W. Cortland (Paulina), Bucktown, (773) 862-5263
Contemporary American
Corkage: $15

JAPONAIS
600 W. Chicago (Larrabee), River West, (312) 822-9600
Japanese
Corkage: $25

KABUKI
2473 N. Clark (St. James), Lincoln Park, (773) 975-2320
Japanese
Corkage: none; wine, beer, sake, spirits allowed

KAZE SUSHI
2032 W. Roscoe (Seeley), Roscoe Village, (773) 327-4860
Japanese
Corkage: $15; wine and sake allowed

KENDALL COLLEGE DINING ROOM
900 N. Branch (Chicago), Goose Island, (312) 752-2328
Contemporary American
Corkage: $10

KIKI'S BISTRO
900 N. Franklin (Walton), Near North, (312) 335-5454
French
Corkage: $20

KOI
624 Davis (Chicago), Evanston, (847) 866-6969
Chinese/Japanese
Corkage: $10

LA FONDA
5350 N. Broadway (Devon), Edgewater, (773) 271-3935
Nuevo Latino
Corkage: $5

Corkage fees are per 750 mL bottle of wine. Only BYO wines to these restaurants (unless beer, spirits, or sake is indicated). Do not bring a wine on the restaurant's list.

LA PETITE FOLIE
1504 E. 55th (Lake Park Ave.), Hyde Park, (773) 493-1394
French
Corkage: $20

LA TACHE
1475 W. Balmoral (Clark), Andersonville, (773) 334-7168
French
Corkage: $15

LAO BEIJING
2138 S. Archer (China Place), Chinatown, (312) 881-0168
Chinese
Corkage: $5

LAO SZE CHUAN
2172 S. Archer (Cermak), Chinatown, (312) 326-5040
Chinese
Corkage: $10

LAS TABLAS
2942 N. Lincoln (Wellington), Lakeview, (773) 871-2414
Colombian
Corkage: $8; none on Mon–Wed

LAWRY'S THE PRIME RIB
100 E. Ontario (Rush), Near North, (312) 787-5000
Steakhouse
Corkage: $15

LE COLONIAL
937 N. Rush (Walton), Near North, (312) 255-0088
Vietnamese
Corkage: $20

LE TITI DE PARIS
1015 W. Dundee (Kennicott), Arlington Heights, (847) 506-0222
French
Corkage: $35

LE VICHYSSOIS
220 W. Route 120 (Lake Drive S.), Lakemoor, (815) 385-8221
French
Corkage: $20

LEE WING WAH
2147 S. China Place (Cermak), Chinatown, (312) 808-1628
Chinese
Corkage: $5 per table

LEONA'S
3877 N. Elston (Grace), Irving Park, (773) 267-7287
Italian
Corkage: $7

LEONARDO'S RISTORANTE
5657 N. Clark (Hollywood), Edgewater, (773) 561-5028
Italian
Corkage: $15; three-bottle limit

LIPS
3705 N. Southport (Waveland), Lakeview, (773) 248-5477
Japanese
Corkage: $2 per table

LOS MOLES
3140 N. Lincoln (Belmont), Lakeview, (773) 935-9620
Nuevo Latino
Corkage: $8

LOVELLS OF LAKE FOREST
915 S. Waukegan (Gloucester Crossing), Lake Forest,
(847) 234-8013
American
Corkage: $20

Corkage fees are per 750 mL bottle of wine. Only BYO wines to these
restaurants (unless beer, spirits, or sake is indicated). Do not bring a wine
on the restaurant's list.

L20
2300 N. Lincoln Park West (Belden), Lincoln Park,
(773) 868-0002
Seafood
Corkage: $40

LUCKY PLATTER
514 Main (Chicago), Evanston, (847) 869-4064
Eclectic
Corkage: $1.50 per person

LULA'S
2537 N. Kedzie (Wrightwood), Logan Square, (773) 489-9554
Eclectic
Corkage: $15

MAGNOLIA CAFÉ
1224 W. Wilson (Magnolia), Uptown, (773) 728-8785
Contemporary American
Corkage: $15

MAIJEAN
30 S. Prospect (Park), Clarendon Hills, (630) 794-8900
French
Corkage: $25

MAMA THAI
1112 W. Madison (Harlem), Oak Park, (708) 386-0100
Thai
Corkage: $7 for wine, $1 per 16-oz. beer

MARCHE
833 W. Randolph (Green), West Loop, (312) 226-8399
French
Corkage: $25

MAYAN SOL
3830 W. Lawrence (Avers), Albany Park, (773) 539-4398
Latin
Corkage: none for 1–2 bottles of wine, $6 thereafter

MAZA

2748 N. Lincoln (Diversey), Lakeview, (773) 929-9600
Mediterranean
Corkage: $8; wine and beer allowed

MEIJI

623 W. Randolph (Jefferson), West Loop, (312) 887-9999
Japanese
Corkage: $15; none on Mondays

MESON SABIKA

1025 Aurora Ave. (Devonshire), Naperville, (630) 983-3000
Tapas
Corkage: $25

MEXIQUE

1529 W. Chicago (Ashland), West Town, (312) 850-0288
French/Mexican
Corkage: $15

MIRAI SUSHI

2020 W. Division (Damen), Wicker Park, (773) 862-8500
Japanese
Corkage: $20

MIRAMAR

301 Waukegan (Temple), Highwood, (847) 433-1078
French
Corkage: $30

MK

868 N. Franklin (Chestnut), Near North, (312) 482-9179
Contemporary American
Corkage: $35; one-bottle limit

MUNDIAL COCINA MESTIZA

1640 W. 18th (Marshfield), Pilsen, (312) 491-9908
Mexican
Corkage: $10; one-bottle limit

Corkage fees are per 750 mL bottle of wine. Only BYO wines to these
restaurants (unless beer, spirits, or sake is indicated). Do not bring a wine
on the restaurant's list.

NICHE
14 S. Third (Route 38), Geneva, (630) 262-1000
Eclectic
Corkage: $15 on weekdays, $25 on weekends

NICK'S FISHMARKET
10275 W. Higgins (Mannheim), Rosemont, (847) 298-8200
Seafood
Corkage: $15

NORTH POND
2610 N. Cannon, Lincoln Park, (773) 477-5845
Contemporary American
Corkage: $25; one-bottle limit

NOYES ST. CAFÉ
828 W. Noyes (Sherman), Evanston, (847) 475-8683
Greek/Italian
Corkage: $7

ONE SIXTY BLUE
1400 W. Randolph (Ogden), West Loop, (312) 850-0303
Eclectic
Corkage: $25; none on last Friday of the month, or "Dust off That Bottle Night"

OPERA
1301 S. Wabash (13th), South Loop, (312) 461-0161
Contemporary Chinese
Corkage: $25

PAPASPIROS
733 Lake (Oak Park Ave.), Oak Park, (708) 358-1700
Greek
Corkage: $10

PARKERS' OCEAN GRILL
1000 31st (Highland), Downers Grove, (630) 960-5700
Seafood
Corkage: $20

PARROT CAGE
7059 S. Shore (70th), South Side, (773) 602-5333
Contemporary American
Corkage: $5

PETE MILLER'S STEAKHOUSE
1557 Sherman (Grove), Evanston, (847) 328-0399
Contemporary American
Corkage: $15

PIAZZA BELLA
2116 W. Roscoe (Leavitt), Roscoe Village, (773) 477-7330
Italian
Corkage: $15

PINGPONG
3322 N. Broadway (Aldine), Lakeview, (773) 281-7575
Pan-Asian
Corkage: $5; wine, sake, and beer allowed

PONZU SUSHI
2407 N. Clark (Fullerton), Lincoln Park, (773) 549-8890
Japanese
Corkage: $2.50 per person

PORT EDWARD RESTAURANT
20 W. Algonquin (River Rd.), Algonquin, (847) 658-5441
Seafood
Corkage: $15

PRAIRIE GRASS CAFÉ
601 Skokie Blvd. (Dundee), Northbrook, (847) 205-4433
Contemporary American
Corkage: $25; none on Mondays

P.S. BANGKOK
3345 N. Clark (Roscoe), Lakeview, (773) 871-7777
Thai
Corkage: $10

Corkage fees are per 750 mL bottle of wine. Only BYO wines to these
restaurants (unless beer, spirits, or sake is indicated). Do not bring a wine
on the restaurant's list.

RAS DASCHEN
5846 N. Broadway (Rosedale), Edgewater, (773) 506-9601
Ethiopian
Corkage: $7

RAW BAR
3720 N. Clark (Waveland), Lakeview, (773) 348-7291
Persian/Seafood
Corkage: $7

RED LIGHT
820 W. Randolph (Green), West Loop, (312) 733-8880
Pan-Asian
Corkage: $25

RESTAURANT TAKASHI
1952 N. Damen (Armitage), Bucktown, (773) 772-6170
Japanese
Corkage: $25

RINGO
2507–09 N. Lincoln (Altgeld), Lincoln Park, (773) 248-5788
Japanese
Corkage: $3.50 for wine, $5.50 for 750 mL bottle of spirits, $1
per 16-oz. beer plus $1 per person

RIOS D'SUDAMERICA
2010 W. Armitage (Damen), Bucktown, (773) 276-0170
Peruvian
Corkage: $10; none on Mon–Wed

ROSAL'S
1154 W. Taylor (Racine), University Village/Little Italy,
(312) 243-2357
Italian
Corkage: $25

ROYIN
1930 Central (Green Bay Rd.), Evanston, (847) 332-2203
Pan-Asian
Corkage: $5

SANOOK
2845 W. Irving Park (Francisco), North Center, (773) 463-7229
Japanese/Thai
Corkage: $5

SCOOZI!
410 W. Huron (Sedgwick), River North, (312) 943-5900
Italian
Corkage: $15; none on Wednesdays

1776
397 Virginia St. (Route 14), Crystal Lake, (815) 356-1776
Contemporary American
Corkage: $15

SHAW'S CRAB HOUSE
21 E. Hubbard (State), Near North, (312) 527-2722
Seafood
Corkage: $20

SHINE
756 W. Webster (Halsted), Lincoln Park, (773) 296-0101
Pan-Asian
Corkage: $15

SIAM PASTA
809 Dempster (Elmwood), Evanston, (847) 328-4614
Thai
Corkage: $7

SIAM THAI
1639–43 E. 55th (Cornell), Hyde Park, (773) 324-9296
Thai
Corkage: none

SIBONEY CUBAN CUISINE
2165 N. Western (Palmer), Bucktown, (773) 904-7210
Cuban
Corkage: $5 per person

Corkage fees are per 750 mL bottle of wine. Only BYO wines to these
restaurants (unless beer, spirits, or sake is indicated). Do not bring a wine
on the restaurant's list.

SILVER SEAFOOD
4829 N. Broadway (Lawrence), Uptown, (773) 784-0668
Chinese
Corkage: $5

SILVER SPOON
710 N. Rush (Huron), River North, (312) 944-7100
Thai
Corkage: none downstairs, $15 upstairs at the sushi bar

SMITH & WOLLENSKY
318 N. State (Kinzie), Near North, (312) 670-9900
Steakhouse
Corkage: $35

SOCCA
3301 N. Clark (Aldine), Lakeview, (773) 248-1155
French/Italian
Corkage: $20; none on Mondays

SOL DE MEXICO
3018 N. Cicero (Wellington), Northwest Side, (773) 282-4119
Mexican
Corkage: $10

SOLGA
5828 N. Lincoln (Peterson), West Rogers Park, (773) 728-0802
Korean BBQ
Corkage: $5

SOUTH COAST
1700 S. Michigan (17th), South Loop, (312) 662-1700
Japanese
Corkage: $20

SOUTHPORT GROCERY
3552 N. Southport (Addison), Lakeview, (773) 665-0100
Contemporary American
Corkage: $5, waived if wine is bought at Southport Grocery

S-PARAGON
503 Main St. (Hinman), Evanston, (847) 332-2302
Pan-Asian
Corkage: $15; none on Saturdays

SUGARTOAD
2139 CityGate Lane (Ferry Rd.), Naperville, (630) 778-8623
Contemporary American
Corkage: $15; two-bottle limit

SUN WAH BAR-B-Q
5041 N. Broadway (Argyle), Uptown, (773) 769-1254
Chinese
Corkage: $3 for wine, $1 per 16-oz. beer (negotiable with large groups)

SUSHI LUXE
5201 N. Clark (Foster), Andersonville, (773) 334-0770
Japanese
Corkage: $2

SYMPHONY'S CAFÉ
1945 Central (Green Bay Rd.), Evanston, (847) 475-1200
Italian
Corkage: $3 per person

TANK
4514 N. Lincoln (Sunnyside), Lincoln Square, (773) 769-2600
Japanese
Corkage: $20

TAPAS BARCELONA
1615 Chicago (Davis), Evanston, (847) 866-9900
Spanish
Corkage: $15

Corkage fees are per 750 mL bottle of wine. Only BYO wines to these restaurants (unless beer, spirits, or sake is indicated). Do not bring a wine on the restaurant's list.

TERRAGUSTO
340 W. Armitage (Orleans), Lincoln Park, (773) 281-7200
Italian
Corkage: $3 per person

THAI SOOKDEE
1016 Church (Maple), Evanston, (847) 866-8012
Thai
Corkage: $5

THREE HAPPINESS
2130 S. Wentworth (22nd), Chinatown, (312) 791-1228
Chinese
Corkage: $5

TIN FISH
18201 S. Harlem (Oak Park Ave.), Tinley Park, (708) 532-0200
Seafood
Corkage: $5 per person per bottle

TIPAROS
1540 N. Clark (North), Old Town, (312) 712-9900
Thai
Corkage: $5

TOPO GIGIO
1516 N. Wells (North), Old Town, (312) 266-9355
Italian
Corkage: $15

TOPOLOBAMPO
445 N. Clark (Illinois), Near North, (312) 661-1434
Mexican
Corkage: $25

TRATTORIA ROMA
1535 N. Wells (North), Old Town, (312) 664-7907
Italian
Corkage: $15

TRIAD SUSHI
1933 S. Indiana (Cullerton), South Loop, (312) 225-8833
Japanese
Corkage: none

TUB TIM THAI
4927 Oakton (Skokie Blvd.), Skokie, (847) 675-8424
Thai
Corkage: $3 per person

UNION
1245 Chicago (Dempster), Evanston, (847) 475-2400
Italian
Corkage: $20

VA PENSIERO
1566 Oak (Davis), Evanston, (847) 475-7779
Italian
Corkage: $15

VIE
4471 Lawn (Burlington), Western Springs, (708) 246-2082
Contemporary American
Corkage: $20; none if the vintage is more than 25 years old;
none on Tuesdays for parties of six or less

VINCI
1732 N. Halsted (Willow), Lincoln Park, (312) 266-1199
Italian
Corkage: $15; none if the vintage is more than 10 years old

WAKAMONO
3317 N. Broadway (Aldine), Lakeview, (773) 296-6800
Japanese
Corkage: $5 for wine, sake, or six-pack of beer

YANG
28 E. Roosevelt (State), South Loop, (312) 986-1688
Chinese
Corkage: $2

Corkage fees are per 750 mL bottle of wine. Only BYO wines to these
restaurants (unless beer, spirits, or sake is indicated). Do not bring a wine
on the restaurant's list.

YUMMY GOURMET
1255 E. Rand Rd. (Thomas), Arlington Heights, (847) 253-0319
Chinese/Japanese
Corkage: $5

ZEN NOODLE
1852 W. North (Wolcott), Wicker Park, (773) 276-8300
Pan-Asian
Corkage: none for a limited time "during the recession"; wine and
beer allowed

Wine & Spirits Stores

CHICAGO

Wine & Spirits Stores A–Z

ARMANETTI TOWN
10000 S. Western (100th), Beverly
The Gibbons family has owned and operated this neighborhood liquor store for over 25 years. To keep up with evolving tastes, they now carry a wider variety of beers and wines, from PBR to IPAs and large-production to small-batch, boutique wines. They also carry wines (and meads) from nearby Bev Art Brewing and Winemaker Supply, where locals learn the art of winemaking and brewing.
(773) 239-2800, Mon–Fri 10–10, Sat 9–10, Sun 11–7

ARMANETTI WINE SHOPPE AND BEVERAGE MART
3530 N. Lincoln (Addison), Roscoe Village
Under new ownership since the Armanettis sold in 2006, this shop is packed with a highly praised beer selection (imported and domestic microbrews), premium spirits, and about 800 wines. A sommelier is on staff to help give pairing recommendations. Free wine tastings every Saturday from 2–6 and free beer tastings every Friday from 5–8.
(773) 529-0288, armanettis.com, Mon–Fri 11–9, Sat 10–9, Sun 11–5 Ⓟ

AVONDALE ARMANETTI BEVERAGE MART
3018 N. Milwaukee (Wellington), Logan Square
Founded in 1956 by Norman Feinmehl, this independently owned store is now run by his son, Mark. The area's predominantly Polish population heavily influences the selection here; there are two aisles packed with Polish and other imported beer, and one entire wall features vodkas from all over the world. Most of the wines are from California, Australia, and Italy and average about $10 a bottle.
(773) 227-1793, armanetti.com, Mon–Wed 9–9, Thurs–Sat 9–10, Sun 11–9

BINNY'S BEVERAGE DEPOT

There has been a lot of change in Chicago's retail beverage landscape since the last edition of *BYOB Chicago*, which was published in late 2006. Some retail kings have faltered while boutique shops have flourished. Throughout it all, Binny's has steadily risen to the top with a reliable business concept that truly leaves no customer behind. In business since 1947, Binny's has earned a respectable rep in this town, and locals know they can depend on Binny's now-22 superstores for their wine, beer, spirits, accessory (and cigar) needs. This retailer equally caters to collectors seeking cellar finds and futures to those searching for a New World value wine from Australia or South America. All locations offer free and paid tastings and educational events for wine, beer, and spirits enthusiasts, presented by some of the world's major producers and distributors; see their Web site for a schedule. BYOB diners can shop online then pick up their order or have it delivered. Call each location for hours.

binnys.com

Chicago

South Loop: 1132 S. Jefferson (Roosevelt), (312) 768-4400

River North: 213 W. Grand (Wells), (312) 332-0012

Lakeview: 3000 N. Clark (Wellington), (773) 935-9400

Hyde Park: 1531 E. 53rd (Lake Park Ave.), (773) 324-5000

Suburbs

Algonquin: 844 Randall (Narnish, next to Walmart), (847) 458-2470

Buffalo Grove: 124 McHenry Rd. (Lake Cook & 83), (847) 459-2200

Des Plaines: 767 W. Golf (Market Place Shopping Center), (847) 956-1000

Elmwood Park: 7330 W. North (74th Ave.), (708) 456-2112

Glen Ellyn: 670 Roosevelt Rd. (Pickwick Place Shopping Center), (630) 545-2550

Glencoe: 71 N. Greenbay Rd. (Hubbard Woods Shopping Center), (847) 835-3900

Highland Park: 153 Skokie Valley Hwy. (Cross Roads Shopping Center), (847) 831-5400

Lake Zurich: 975 S. Rand (Deerpath), (847) 438-1437

McHenry: 4610 W. Elm (on Route 120), (815) 385-3200

Naperville: 790 Royal St. George (Ogden, in Cress Creek Square Shopping Center), (630) 717-0100

Niles: 8935 N. Milwaukee (Ballard), (847) 966-2300

Orland Park: 103A Orland Park Pl. (151st), (708) 226-9902

Plainfield: 12307 S. Route 59, (815) 436-9300

River Grove: 3121 Thatcher (Belmont), (708) 456-7400

Schaumburg: 323 W. Golf (Valley Lake Dr.), (847) 882-6000

Skokie: 5100 W. Dempster (Le Claire), (847) 674-4200

St. Charles: 1950 Lincoln Hwy., (630) 377-1671

Willowbrook: 6920 S. Route 83 (Plainfield Rd.), (630) 654-0988

THE BOTTLE SHOP
1138 Central (Wilmette), Wilmette
Jokingly referred to as Amy's Wine House (Amy LaFontant is the owner), this place is so much fun to visit, it's hard to leave. Anti-corporate and completely unpretentious, The Bottle Shop finds rare, small-batch wines from all over the world and opens some of them on Saturdays (and occasionally during the week) for customers to sample. They've added a wine bar that serves wines by the glass and bottle, small plates, and gelato.
(847) 256-7777, thebottleshop.net, Mon–Sat 10–7, Sun 12–5

CABERNET & CO.
434 N. Main St. (Duane), Glen Ellyn
This is the only Cabernet & Co. store left (owners sold the Oak Park and Naperville locations), but the same concept is in play: a whittled-down, easy-to-navigate selection of both domestic and imported boutique wines at affordable prices. The shop hosts several tastings and classes throughout the year; see their Web site or call for a schedule.
(630) 469-2644, cabernetco.com, Mon–Wed 10–7, Thurs 10–9, Fri 10–8, Sat 9–7, Sun 12–4

CELLAR RAT WINE SHOP
1811 W. North (Wood), Wicker Park
This neighborhood shop stocks hand-selected boutique wines, most under $20, and a small supply of microbrews and accessories. Owner Dean Schlabowske (Sam's, Wine Discount Center), who also slings guitar for local band Waco Brothers, always has a few bottles open for tasting any day of the week and carries a generous selection of organic wines.
(773) 489-2728, cellarratchicago.com, Mon–Sat 11–9, Sun 12–5

CONVITO ITALIANO
151 Sheridan (Plaza del Lago), Wilmette
The emphasis of their selection is on Italian wines, but there are also small-batch choices from all over the globe at this gourmet food and wine market. Have lunch or dinner next door at The Convito Café, where you can bring a bottle purchased at the wine shop for a $10 corkage fee.
(847) 251-3654, convitocafeandmarket.com, Mon–Fri 10–6:30, Sat 9:30–6, Sun 11–5

THE CORK
2720 S. Harlem (Longcommon), Riverside
The staff at this tucked-away shop (across the street from the Berwyn library) are foodies at heart and happy to offer recommendations for the perfect bottle for various BYOB destinations. Beer geeks will rejoice at the 350+ choices on hand, and there's a wide array of premium spirits and wines (mostly boutique) representing all corners of the globe to round out the selection.
(708) 443-9463, thecorkwineshop.com, Mon 12–8, Tues–Thurs 12–9, Fri–Sat 12–10, Sun 12–6

DICARLO'S ARMANETTI
515 N. Western (Grand), West Town
Exteriors can be deceiving, as is the case with this hidden treasure. DiCarlo's stocks several aisles of carefully chosen boutique wines from around the world, and helpful wine experts are on hand to assist you with your selection. There's also a growing selection of microbrews and an extensive variety of tequila and South American spirits and beers to cater to the neighborhood. Call for their schedule of events and tastings.
(312) 226-4600, armanetti.com, Mon–Sat 9–9, Sun 11–6 Ⓟ

DRINKS OVER DEARBORN
650 N. Dearborn (Erie), River North
Kyle McHugh opened this environmentally friendly boutique shop in 2008 to cater to more refined tastes with small-batch wines, beers, and spirits that are surprisingly affordable. McHugh, a self-proclaimed "boozehound," strives to find the best local producers (Goose Island, Lynfred Winery, Half Acre, North Shore Distillery) across all categories. The shop is on the second floor, above The Joynt.
(312) 337-9463, drinksoverdearborn.com, Mon–Sat 11–9, Sun 11–5

FINE WINE BROKERS
4621 N. Lincoln (Wilson), Lincoln Square
This established fine-wine shop has expanded its selection of boutique, organic wines from France, Italy, Spain, Australia, and the United States to include South American and South African vinos; microbrews; small-batch bourbons, ryes, and Scotches; and artisanal meats and cheeses. Drop by on Saturdays, when they host free public wine tastings from 1–4.
(773) 989-8166, fwbchicago.com, Mon–Fri 12–7:30, Sat 10–6:30, Sun 12–4

FOODSTUFFS
338 Park (Green Bay Rd.), Glencoe
North Shore–based gourmet grocer Foodstuffs (think small-scale Whole Foods) has four stores, but this original location—open since 1979—is the only one that carries wine. Alongside specialty groceries, prepared foods, and cheeses, find boutique wines (including some dessert and sparkling). Most are in the $10–$30 range; all are selected with convenience in mind. Located near Metra's Glencoe stop, so you can tote a bottle to Ravinia (the grandest BYOB of them all).
(847) 835-5105, foodstuffs.com, Mon–Fri 10–6:30, Sat 9–5, Sun 10–5

FOREMOST LIQUORS
1040 W. Argyle (Kenmore), Uptown
This strip of Argyle, from Broadway to Sheridan, is known to many as "Little Saigon," with its myriad Vietnamese eateries. Today, this strip is nearly 100% BYOB—great news for Foremost, one of the only places to sell alcohol in the immediate area. The inventory is several notches above a corner liquor store's, so expect Dogfish 60 Minute IPA next to Miller Lite, and small-batch Malbec next to Barefoot Cellars Chardonnay. Spirits, liqueurs, and mixers are also available.
(773) 989-0808, Mon–Sat 9:30–10, Sun 11:30–8

FOX & OBEL FOOD MARKET
401 E. Illinois (McClurg), Streeterville
This 22,000-square-foot space is a culinary playground, offering a bounty of fine pastries, freshly baked artisan breads, a fromagerie, prepared gourmet foods, and more. Its fine wine shop carries rare wines, many of them estate-bottled, and premium spirits, imported beers, and domestic microbrews. Special bonus: There's free two-hour parking with $20 purchase and free curbside service to help with your haul. Free tastings every Saturday from 2–4.
(312) 410-7301, foxandobel.com, 6–12 daily

GALLERIA LIQUEURS
1559 N. Wells (North), Old Town
The front of this charming store stocks 200 bottles under $15 and a large supply of accessories for grab-and-go customers. But walk toward the back for an ample supply of high-end, Old World fine wines and rare Champagnes. They will deliver to nearby BYOBs for a $3 fee; just call and they'll send a bottle right over. Free wine tastings every Saturday from 3–6.
(312) 867-7070, Mon–Thurs 9–12, Fri–Sat 9–1a, Sun 11–12

GALLERIA LIQUEURS
3409 N. Southport (Roscoe), Lakeview
This newer, larger, second location is similar in concept to the Old Town original (late-night hours, fine wines) but caters to a younger demographic with a larger microbrew selection and about 200 red and white wines under $10. Brown Line commuters can walk directly into the store from the Southport station and buy a bottle on the way home. Free wine tastings every Saturday from 3–6; beer or spirits tastings are held every other Friday. Call the store for details.
(773) 857-6200, Mon–Thurs 9–12, Fri–Sat 9–1a, Sun 11–12

GENTILE'S
1160 W. Taylor (Racine), University Village/Little Italy
Flavio Gentile, who also owns Printer's Row Wine Shop, opened this second location on a block of Taylor Street that is packed with casual BYOBs (see the BYOB Restaurants by Location index in the back of the book for a list). Gentile carries an extensive selection of microbrews and boutique wines from all over the world, including an ample supply of BYOB-ready chilled bottles. Friday night tastings rotate between the two locations.
(312) 850-9463, printersrowwine.com, Mon–Wed 12–10, Thurs–Sat 12–11, Sun 12–8

THE GODDESS & GROCER
1646 N. Damen (Wabansia), Bucktown
Owner Debra Sharpe's (Feast, Cru) gourmet prepared foods and grocery shop has become an anchor in the bustling Wicker Park/ Bucktown area. The wine choices keep expanding, with Feast's Bucktown buyer stocking the popular 20-under-$20 selections and other fine wines. Sharpe strives for local producers (Metropolitan Brewing, Seedling Farms) and comps customers for one bottle with every 12 purchased. Plenty of chilled options available.
(773) 342-3200, goddessandgrocer.com, Mon–Fri 6–9, Sat–Sun 7–8

THE GODDESS & GROCER
25 E. Delaware (State), Gold Coast
Sharpe extends her culinary emporium to the Gold Coast area with this second location (a third on Elston offers prepared foods, no wine). Sharpe executes the same concept—prepared foods, specialty groceries, wine, beer—but with a larger wine selection, some in the high-end category to suit the neighborhood. The wine buyer from Feast's Gold Coast location (next door, formerly Cru) selects wines for this shop, so you're in expert hands.
(312) 896-2600, goddessandgrocer.com, 8–9 daily

THE GOURMET GRAPE
3530 N. Halsted (Brompton), Lakeview
In the neighborhood since 2003, Gourmet Grape caters to all tastes and budgets, from locals seeking a bottle of wine under $15 to oenophiles seeking higher education through focused tastings and classes. This elegant shop has a wide selection of gifts and accessories, so this is the place to pick up some fine stemware if you're heading to a BYOB that has none.
(773) 388-0942, gourmetgrape.com, Mon closed, Tues–Sat 11–9, Sun 12–6

THE HOUSE OF GLUNZ
1206 N. Wells (Division), Old Town
Since 1888, the Glunz family has served the community with
fine wines, handcrafted beers (mostly Belgian and German), rare
spirits, and educational events. Take advantage of their "open
house" tastings every Saturday from 2–6, when they feature new
arrivals, seasonal specials, and end-of-bin deals.
(312) 642-3000, thehouseofglunz.com, Mon–Fri 10–8, Sat 10–7,
Sun 2–5

HOUSE RED
7403 W. Madison (Circle), Forest Park
This place has a piano, comfy armchairs, and several musicians
on staff, so you never know what will happen. They also seek
the best boutique, biodynamic wines from sustainable wineries
all over the world. Plans for a wine lounge with self-serve finger
foods and wines by the glass (from their self-serve tasting station)
were in the works at press time.
(708) 771-7733, house-red.com, Mon closed, Tues 12–8,
Wed–Thurs 11–8, Fri 12–9, Sat 11–7, Sun 12–5

HOWARD'S WINE CELLAR
1244 W. Belmont (Lakewood), Lakeview
Howard Silverman opened this one-man shop, which is stocked
from floor to ceiling with mostly imported wines (about 70% of
the stock, no beer or spirits), in 1997, after spending over 20
years at Sam's Wine & Spirits. Silverman's longtime, established
relationships in the wine industry mean competitive prices on
even rare and small-batch selections. He caters to all tastes and
budgets, though, from locals looking for a $10 bottle to collectors
searching for an elusive case of Bordeaux. Free tastings held every
Saturday from 12–4. Get on the store's e-mail list for specials and
new releases.
(773) 248-3766, Sun–Mon closed, Tues–Fri 10–7, Sat 9–5 Ⓟ

IN FINE SPIRITS
5418 N. Clark (Balmoral), Andersonville
Friendly service and New World value wines distinguish this neighborhood boutique shop. Owners Shane and Jill Kissack have a fondness for peculiar varietals and love steering customers to one of their latest discoveries, many of which fall below $12. Besides an exciting wine selection, browse the shop's many craft beers (Three Floyd's, Founder's, Arcadia, Two Brothers), premium spirits, and sakes. Free tastings every other Saturday and first Friday of the month (check Web site for details).
(773) 506-9463, infinespirits.com, Sun–Mon 12–7, Tues–Fri 12–9, Sat 11–9

JUICY WINE CO.
694 N. Milwaukee (Huron), River West
Owner Rodney Alex has forged his unique signature on Chicago with an unmatched business concept that's part lounge, part cheese shop, part retail store, part neighborhood hangout and Sunday brunch spot. The wine shop offers a carefully selected variety of domestic and imported small-batch vinos at all price points and a growing selection of beer.
(312) 492-6620, juicywine.com, Mon–Thurs 4–1, Fri–Sat 4–2, Sun 11–3 (brunch), 4–12

JUST GRAPES
560 W. Washington (Clinton), West Loop
This burgeoning West Loop store hosts educational, fun, interactive classes for budding wine enthusiasts at its on-site classroom, has complimentary tastings every Saturday from 2–4, and boasts the city's only self-serve wine tasting machine. Many restaurants in the area waive corkage for wine purchased here; ask staff for current information.
(312) 627-9463, justgrapes.net, Mon–Thurs 11–7, Fri 11–8, Sat 12–6, Sun closed

KAFKA WINE CO.
3325 N. Halsted (Buckingham), Lakeview
Located in the heart of BYOB central, Kafka is the place to go for
value wines, or high-quality wines that don't fetch a high price
tag. There are over 250 bottles available for less than $15, so you
can stock up on several for the night without blowing your budget. The staff here are experts at wine and food pairing, so bring
the menu from your chosen BYOB for some reliable recommendations. Or, attend their monthly food and wine pairing classes, and
soon you'll be the expert.
(773) 975-9463, kafkawine.com, Mon–Sat 12–10, Sun 12–7

KNIGHTSBRIDGE WINE SHOPPE
824 Sunset Ridge (Skokie Blvd.), Northbrook
This beautifully designed, elegant wine shop is a little tricky to
find (located just off the Dundee exit on the Edens Expressway)
but worth the trouble. Knightsbridge features an experienced staff,
superb service, and rare, world-class wines. Most of the selection is
$50–$100 and up, though rare finds like a 2005 Petrus fetch over
$4K. Their culinary and wine-related book selection is unmatched.
If a trip to Northbrook is not in your plans, shop online and have
your order delivered.
(847) 498-9300, knightsbridgewine.com, Mon–Fri 10–7, Sat
10–6, Sun closed

LUSH WINE AND SPIRITS
2232 W. Roscoe (Bell), Roscoe Village
1257 S. Halsted (Roosevelt), University Village/Little Italy
1412 W. Chicago (Noble), West Town
When it comes to describing the vibe at Mitch Einhorn's boutique
wine shops, the tongue-in-cheek name—Lush—says it all. The
staff are laid back but passionate about great wine and helping
customers find a rare, small-batch selection. Employees (who
call themselves "lushies") are also avid foodies who frequent
the city's BYOBs, and are eager to hook up their customers with
food-friendly wines or microbrews. Einhorn (Twisted Spoke), a
bourbon aficionado, also stocks an assortment of rare bourbons
and handcrafted spirits. Free tastings every Sunday from 2–5.
Roscoe Village: (773) 281-8888, 12–10 daily
University Village/Little Italy: (312) 738-1900, 12–10 daily
West Town: (312) 666-6900, 12–10 daily
lushwineandspirits.com

THE NOBLE GRAPE
802 N. Bishop (Chicago), West Town
The Noble Grape joined the booming West Town community in summer 2009 and established itself as a friendly, corner store with moderately priced boutique wines (most under $30). They're also passionate about finding the best craft brews (Gumball Head) and premium sakes and spirits. They even sell DIY wine storage units, so you can proudly display your wine collection at home. Expect tastings and events from small producers; check the Web site for a schedule.
(312) 846-1204, noblegrape.net, Mon–Thurs 12–9, Sat 12–12, Sun 12–8

OLIVIA'S MARKET
2014 W. Wabansia (Damen), Bucktown
One of the first gourmet grocery stores to hit this double stroller–filled neighborhood, Olivia's Market has expanded its selection over the years. There are now several imported and domestic boutique wines, microbrews, and premium sakes, all selected with convenience in mind. Owners were smart to get multiple loading zones in front of the store, making a pit stop at Damen and Wabansia (arguably one of the most hazardous and congested intersections in the city) possible.
(773) 227-4220, oliviasmarket.com, 8–9 daily

PASTORAL ARTISAN CHEESE, BREAD & WINE
2945 N. Broadway (Oakdale), Lakeview
This intimate shop carries a high-quality selection of artisanal cheeses, breads, gourmet grocery items, and distinctive, small-batch wines for discriminating tastes. Sommelier Jan Henrichsen (formerly at Bin 36) selects the wines, which are all food-friendly and ideal for pairing with the cheeses sold in the shop or at the dozens of nearby BYOBs.
(773) 472-4781, pastoralartisan.com, Mon–Fri 11–8, Sat 11–7, Sun 11–6

PASTORAL ARTISAN CHEESE, BREAD & WINE
53 E. Lake (State), the Loop
This second location offers the same types of gourmet foods and
wines as the original in Lakeview, but the larger space accommodates a wider wine selection. Many of Pastoral's fine wines are
screw-capped, making them perfect for taking to a BYOB; if you
don't finish the bottle, just twist the cap back on, put it in the
trunk or a resealable bag (per Illinois' open container law), and
take it home. Classes are held at both stores once a month; check
their Web site for details.
(312) 658-1250, pastoralartisan.com, Mon–Fri 10:30–8, Sat–Sun
11–6

PASTORAL ARTISAN CHEESE, BREAD & WINE
131 N. Clinton (Lake), the Loop
Pastoral planted this third locale in the French Market, a group
of food vendors that hawk mostly organic goods within the
MetraMarket development surrounding the Ogilvie Transporta-
tion Center. Expect the same assortment of small-batch wines,
artisan cheeses, and gourmet groceries.
pastoralartisan.com, Mon–Sat 10–7, Sun closed

PERMAN WINE SELECTIONS
802 W. Washington (Halsted), Greek Town
Owner Craig Perman says it best when it comes to describing his
one-man shop: it's clean, compact, and easy to shop. A Portland,
Oregon, native, Perman (Sam's, Alinea, Avec, Bluebird) carries
his favorite boutique wines at competitive prices. He works very
closely with The Grocery Bistro (BYOB next door) and offers
several suggestions based on their current menu. Several chilled
beers, wines available.
(312) 666-4417, permanwine.com, Mon–Fri 12–9, Sat 11–9, Sun
closed

THE POISON CUP
1128 W. Armitage (Seminary), Lincoln Park
Nothing sounds more complementary than fine wine and art, unless you throw artisan chocolate and cheese into the mix. Did I also mention free wine tastings every Tuesday from 6–8? This beautiful shop carries wines that average $25–$30 a bottle, all sourced from small producers, and features rotating artist exhibits. Take your receipt to Geja's and they'll waive your corkage or take $25 off your bill with purchase of two premier dinners.
(773) 935-1325, poisoncup.com, Mon closed, Tues–Fri 1–9, Sat 11–9, Sun 12–5

PRINTER'S ROW WINE SHOP
719 S. Dearborn (Polk), South Loop
Formerly an old pharmacy, Printer's Row Wine Shop (same owners as Gentile's) serves a growing neighborhood of condo owners and businesses. There's a good selection of chilled microbrews (Dogfish, New Belgium, Great Lakes) and boutique wines, many of which you can try before you buy. Complimentary tastings every other Friday.
(312) 663-9314, printersrowwine.com, Mon–Wed 11–10, Thurs–Sat 11–11, Sun 2–9

PROVENANCE FOOD AND WINE
2528 N. California (Logan Blvd.), Logan Square
Owner Tracy Kellner couldn't find a decent bottle of wine in her Logan Square neighborhood, so in 2006 she opened a place that offers just that. Kellner's boutique shop, which focuses on affordable, everyday wines from $10–$25, has hit its stride with the locals, who also devour her gourmet grocery items and other treats. Wine tastings every Saturday from 3–6.
(773) 384-0699, provenancefoodandwine.com, Mon 12–8, Tues–Sat 12–9, Sun 12–7

PROVENANCE FOOD AND WINE
2312 W. Leland (Western), Lincoln Square
When Bouffe (the cheese shop formerly in this space) closed, owner Tracy Kellner grabbed the opportunity for a second location and opened this shop in 2007. Kellner offers a slightly wider selection of cheeses but essentially the same product mix at this smaller space, which is steps from the Brown Line's Western stop. Free wine tastings every Thursday from 6–8.
(773) 784-2314, provenancefoodandwine.com, Mon closed, Tues–Fri 12–8, Sat 11–8, Sun 12–7

QUE SYRAH
3726 N. Southport (Grace), Lakeview
This neighborhood shop carried more high-end wines when it opened in 2002, but new owners have since switched the focus to affordable, small-production wines (there are 70 under $12) from around the globe. Staff will hand-deliver a bottle to Tango Sur, a BYOB across the street, or take 10% off your purchase if you're dining at Lips (see "Restaurants That Allow BYOB for Corkage Fees of $0–$50"). Check out their ample supply of gifts and accessories, including BYOB cases, stemware, and Lolita glasses. Free wine tastings every first Saturday of the month from 3–7.
(773) 871-8888, quesyrahwine.com, Mon 11–8, Tues–Sat 11–9, Sun 12–7

RANDOLPH WINE CELLARS
1415 W. Randolph (Ogden), West Town
Located at the western portal of Randolph Street's restaurant row, the wines at this boutique shop are given TLC with proper storage (i.e., at the appropriate temperature under lighting that won't compromise the wine). Seasoned sommeliers and wine judges are on staff to help select a wine for the night's BYOB, with most choices in the $10–$25 range. Beer, sake, spirits also available. Free tastings every Saturday from 12–6, with discounts on wines tasted that day.
(312) 942-1212, randolphwinecellars.com, Mon–Fri 11–8, Sat 10–8, Sun closed Ⓟ

RAVE WINES
1114 Chicago (Harlem), Oak Park
The staff here have a combined experience of several decades in the wine industry around the world and are incredibly passionate about sharing their discoveries with customers. Feel free to browse their stock online or at their store, where you'll find small-batch wines ranging from $10–$100. Also discover a few microbrews, stemware, and on-site tastings and private events. On Wednesdays, get a case discount on a six-bottle purchase. Sweet.
(708) 383-3803, ravewines.com, Sun–Mon closed, Tues–Sat 10–6

RED & WHITE WINES
1861 N. Milwaukee (Oakley), Wicker Park
This boutique neighborhood wine shop is, like its name, simple, clean, and minimalist. Owners Sean Krainik and Nathan Adams clocked in 20 years apiece in various restaurants (Mod, Tizi Melloul, Bluebird, Brasserie Jo). To them, wine is a natural extension of the meal, and that's how they run their store. Both are familiar with the menus at several BYOBs (Schwa, Mado, Bonsoirée, Coast, Irazu), so they're pros at pairing suggestions. Free tastings Saturdays from 2–5.
(773) 486-4769, redandwhitechicago.com, Mon 2–9, Tues–Thurs 11–10, Fri–Sat 11–11, Sun 12–8

ROGERS PARK FINE WINES & SPIRITS
6733 N. Clark (Columbia), Rogers Park
Owner Henry Younan completely revamped this former corner liquor store (family-owned since 1992) into a destination for boutique wines, craft beers, and premium spirits. Gone is the Yellowtail. In its place are boutique wines from all over the world and brews such as Delirium Tremens and Great Lakes. Wines are merchandised according to Younan's own point system, most within the $10–$20 range.
(773) 761-1906, Sun–Thurs 11–10:30, Fri–Sat 11–11:30

SAM'S WINE & SPIRITS
1720 N. Marcey (Willow), Lincoln Park
2010 Butterfield Rd. (Lloyd), Downers Grove
A private equity firm specializing in food and beverage companies
now owns a majority interest in Sam's, which was founded in
1945 by Sam Rosen. But customers can still count on Sam's
superstore-sized inventory, which weighs in at nearly 8,000
wines, 800 beers, and 2,500 spirits. Access Sam's Web site for
several staff-written articles to enhance the BYOB dining experience, such as how to pair wine with food, how to read a wine
label, and more. For a more hands-on approach to learning, Sam's
Academy offers tastings and classes, mostly at the flagship Lincoln
Park location.
Lincoln Park: (312) 664-4394, Mon–Thurs 9–8, Fri–Sat 9–9, Sun 11–6
Downers Grove: (630) 705-9463, Mon–Sat 10–8, Sun 12–5
samswine.com

SANDBURG WINE CELLAR
1525 N. Clark (North), Old Town
Located in the lower level of a neighborhood grocery store,
Sandburg Wine Cellar is a treasure trove of boutique wines from
all over the world, painstakingly selected by longtime wine buyer
Alan Blum. Recent remodeling gives shoppers a clearer path for
finding the right bottle of wine (or premium spirits or microbrews). If the free loading zones out front are filled, pull into the
garage and park for free (with a $20 minimum purchase).
(312) 337-7537, Mon–Sat 9:30–10, Sun 11–9

SCHAEFER'S
9965 Gross Point Rd. (Old Orchard Rd.), Skokie
Schaefer's was founded in the mid '40s by George Schaefer, in one of the few towns that permitted the sale of alcohol at the time. Throughout the years, this beloved wine, beer, spirits, and specialty foods store was handed down to a second generation, and it grew into one of the area's most prestigious destinations for fine wine. The family decided to sell in 2008, and they were fortunate to find buyer Bill Graham, a neighbor and devoted customer, who plans to retain Schaefer's tradition as a respected landmark with strong ties to the community. So far, the plan seems to be working, as Schaefer's long-term staff are all still there (many of whom have worked there since the '70s and '80s). The store has since been given a much-needed facelift to accommodate its growing wine and specialty liquor selection. Shop online; they offer free delivery to downtown and the northern suburbs.
(847) 677-9463, schaefers.com, Mon–Thurs 9–7, Fri–Sat 9–8, Sun 11–5

SOUTH LOOP WINE CELLAR
1442 S. Michigan (14th), South Loop
This neighborhood wine shop was born the same way many small businesses are: owner Amy Garman couldn't find a decent bottle of wine in her own neighborhood, so she opened a place that could. Garman stocks her streamlined store with a wide variety of varietals and price points; most bottles are priced at $20 and under. There's also a small, handpicked selection of microbrews (Dogfish, Sprecher, Bell's).
(312) 356-0630, southloopwinecellar.com, Mon–Thurs 3–8, Fri–Sat 12–9, Sun 12–5

SOUTHPORT GROCERY
3552 N. Southport (Addison), Lakeview
Is it a wine shop, a specialty foods store, or a café offering contemporary comfort food? All three, actually. Owner/chef Lisa Santos carefully chooses domestic specialty foods for her small grocery, designed with budding cooks and chefs in mind, as well as a selection of 20 wines under $20 (mostly domestic) and a few bubblies and microbrews. Purchase a bottle from the grocery and bring it to the café for lunch or weekend brunch and they'll waive the $5 corkage fee.
(773) 665-0100, southportgrocery.com, Mon–Fri 7–4, Sat 8–5, Sun 8–4

TASTE FOOD & WINE
1506 Jarvis (Greenview), Rogers Park

A small group of closely knit friends opened this European-style wine and specialty foods/cheese shop in the center of the Jarvis Square neighborhood. Browse the treats and artisan cheeses to your heart's content, then choose from the New and Old World wines, handful of microbrews, or spirits. Now that there are so many BYOBs in Rogers Park, you have several excuses to stop by. Free tastings on Friday evenings.

(773) 761-3663, tastefoodandwine.com, Mon 12–9, Tues closed, Wed–Sat 12–9, Sun 12–6

A TASTE OF VINO
24 W. Chicago (Lincoln), Hinsdale
27 S. Prospect, Clarendon Hills
821 W. Burlington, Western Springs

Tanya Hart has expanded her hybrid wine store/wine bar concept to not one, but three west suburban locations. Hart organizes her wines by style (big, bold, and rich; smooth, luscious, and juicy; light, fresh, and fruity; sticky and sweet; bubbles), which offers a more insightful way of finding the right wine. Not content with offering just vino and nibbles (each wine bar serves full- and half-glass pours and small plates), her Western Springs locale houses a full-service restaurant. Most entrées hover around $20, like the slow-braised lamb shanks with lentils. Pick any bottle off the shelf and drink it at one of the cafés or the restaurant for a $12 corkage fee. Clarendon Hills offers a wine cellar and storage.

Hinsdale: (630) 325-8466, Mon 12–7:30, Tues–Thurs 10–7:30, Fri–Sat 10–11, Sun closed

Clarendon Hills: (630) 323-8444, Sun–Mon closed, Tues–Thurs 11–7:30, Fri–Sat 11–10

Western Springs: (708) 246-8668, Mon closed, Tues–Thurs 11–9, Fri–Sat 11–10, Sun 5–8

atasteofvino.com

TROTTER'S TO GO
1337 W. Fullerton (Wayne), Lincoln Park
This boutique shop specializes in gourmet prepared foods that reflect the celebrated namesake's version of "everyday food." In the retail shop, there are dozens of small-batch wines, color-coded by flavor profile to identify ideal food pairings (a great tool for BYOB diners). Yes, you can still find a magnum of Veuve Clicquot and rare vintages here that fetch triple digits, but the wine buyer has expanded the number of wines in the $15–$30 range, no doubt due to the economy.
(773) 868-6510, charlietrotters.com/togo, Mon–Sat 11–8, Sun 11–6 Ⓟ

TUSCAN MARKET AND SHOP
141 W. Wing (Vail), Arlington Heights
This Italian-American deli/grocery combo has a new owner, who's stirred things up with a new wine bar, a book club, and a generous free tastings schedule (Fridays and Saturdays from 12–6 and third Thursday of the month from 6:30–8:30). The shop's wines rotate frequently and represent quirky, small-batch producers from all over the globe. Take a bottle to their café for $8 above retail or next door to sushi place Himawari, who will waive their corkage fee (for Tuscan customers only).
(847) 392-9700, tuscanwineshop.com, Mon–Thurs 11:30–9, Fri–Sat 11–10, Sun closed

UNCORK IT!
393 E. Illinois (McClurg), Streeterville
George Stellas (Marketplace) offers what he describes as an "upscale selection at warehouse prices." There are over 4,000 wines here, evenly split between large- and small-scale producers, with an ample supply of fine wines stored in the temperature-controlled, aptly named "Wine Room." If it's beer you crave, mix and match a six-pack of imported, domestic, and craft beers. Or order online and save yourself the trip.
(312) 321-9400, uncorkitchicago.com, Mon–Thurs 8–10:30, Fri–Sat 8–11:30, Sun 11–10

VRAI AMOUR WINES
953 W. Webster (Sheffield), Lincoln Park
Father-son team David and Matt Somsky have a true passion
for craft beers and fine wines, and looked for a place in Chicago
(they're originally from Kalamazoo, Michigan) where they could
share this passion with others. Located in the heart of the DePaul
neighborhood, Vrai Amour pays equal attention to craft brews,
especially from Michigan breweries (New Holland, Bell's, Arca-
dia), and seasonal New World wines. Tastings and classes held
weekly; call for a schedule.
(773) 549-9740, vraiamour.com, Mon–Thurs 11–9, Fri–Sat
11–10, Sun 12–6

WEST LAKEVIEW LIQUORS
2156 W. Addison (Leavitt), North Center
This cozy corner store has become one of the country's best-loved
beverage retailers, especially for beer aficionados. Their ability
to offer (and ship) newly released microbrews—before anyone
else grabs them—has no doubt contributed to their "Top 10 Best
Beer Retailers 2009" RateBeer.com rating. Their specialty is rare
imported craft beers (Nøgne, Cantillon, Baird), but expect a wide
variety from domestic craft breweries (Dark Horse, Allagash,
Southern Tier, Three Floyd's) as well. The wine choices are
staggering for such a small shop: over 350 labels from all over the
world, including at least 50 for under $10, while small-batch pro-
ducers such as North Shore Distillery and Old Pappy Van Winkle
dominate the spirits stock. Owners expanded to the former Mail
Boxes Etc. space next door with a specialty foods store, stocked
mostly with locally produced goods (Metropolis Coffee, River
Valley Ranch, Bennison's). Brewers offer samples of their creations
at the store's weekly beer tastings on Fridays from 6–9. Wine
tastings are held every Saturday from 6–9. A few parking spaces
are available at the rear of the store.
(773) 525-1916, westlakeviewliquors.com, Mon–Thurs 10–10,
Fri–Sat 10–11, Sun 11–10 Ⓟ

THE WINE CONSORTIUM
110 E. 23rd (Michigan), South Loop

This communal, multipurpose spot, located near McCormick Place, is a wine shop, wine café, and special events space all under one roof. The creation of Anke Koning, The Wine Consortium carries about 150 wines between $10–$25 from smaller producers ("you'll never find Yellowtail here") and some local microbrews and spirits (Goose Island, North Shore Distillery). The raw, stark space is suitable for art exhibits, and its fully equipped kitchen comes in handy for private events. Enjoy music, wine, and appetizers every first Friday of the month and free tastings on Saturdays from 1–4.

(312) 791-9999, thewineconsortium.com, 11–7 daily

WINE DISCOUNT CENTER
1826 N. Elston (Cortland), Bucktown
311 E. Main (Ela), Barrington
7714 W. Madison (Franklin), Forest Park
1350 Old Skokie Rd., Highland Park

Family owned and operated since 1984, Wine Discount's business model is to pare down occupancy costs with off-the-beaten-path locations, and invest instead in knowledgeable employees who are passionate about fine wine. Experienced staff choose wines from all over the world that score exceptionally high on their 100-point rating system and offer them at bare-bones prices to their customers, who range from beginners to serious collectors. There are several ways to get in on the incredible deals here: join their e-mail list and order online (then pick up at any of their four locations); stop in any Saturday from 12–4 for a free tasting (one of the most popular and educational tastings in Chicagoland); or simply stop in any of their stores and browse the selections, organized by varietal (domestic) and region (import). Friendly staff are always on hand to help find rare deals and limited releases.

Bucktown: (773) 489-3454, Mon–Fri 10–7, Sat 9–6, Sun 12–5
Barrington: (847) 277-0033, Mon–Fri 10–7, Sat 9–5, Sun 12–5
Forest Park: (708) 366-2500, Mon–Sat 9–9, Sun 10–6
Highland Park: (847) 831-1049, Mon–Fri 10–7, Sat 9–5, Sun 12–5
winediscountcenter.com

WINESTYLES
1433 W. Belmont (Southport), Lakeview

WineStyles is a nationwide boutique wine retailer, and several locations have sprouted in Chicagoland. Instead of varietal or region, wines are grouped by flavor profiles such as crisp, silky, rich, nectar, fruity, mellow, etc. But each store has a unique personality that reflects its independent owner and the neighborhood it serves. The Lakeview shop, for example, differentiates itself with a service-oriented approach; customers are given one-on-one, personalized attention as they walk in to peruse the shelves for that perfect bottle. The staff here also specialize in food and wine pairing suggestions. Toward that end, there are free, focused tastings every Thursday from 6–8 and an ongoing Wine Education Series for those seeking more in-depth learning.
(773) 549-2227, winestyles.net/belmont, Mon closed, Tues–Wed 12–8, Thurs–Sat 12–9, Sun 12–8

WINESTYLES
1240 S. Michigan (Roosevelt), South Loop

This retail shop/wine bar combo has become a communal neighborhood place, or what regulars call an "adult coffee shop." There are anywhere from 100–150 wines to choose from, all categorized by WineStyles' trademark flavor profiles. But wait, it gets better. Customers are allowed to BYOF (bring your own food), anything from Jimmy John's to a home-cooked preopera meal to sushi takeout from Ma & I next door, to accompany their wines by the glass or bottle. Live music Thursdays and Fridays.
(312) 431-9999, winestyles.net/southloop, Mon–Wed 12–9, Thurs–Fri 12–11, Sat 11–11, Sun 12–7

WINESTYLES
1741 Sherman (Clark), Evanston

This boutique shop is one of the most BYOB-friendly wine retailers in Chicagoland. There's a collection of menus from local BYOB restaurants near the register, and staff are happy to steer you to the ideal, food-friendly bottle (or three) for your evening meal. There are more than 80 wines on the 6-for-$60 table, which reflects this shop's mission to provide affordable wines from all over the world. Free tastings are held every Thursday from 6–8 and Saturday from 2–4.
(847) 328-4400, winestyles.net/evanston, Mon closed, Tues–Sat 11–8, Sun 12–5

Indexes

BYOB Restaurants by Location

City

ALBANY PARK
Big Pho
Brasa Roja
Cousin's Incredible Vitality
D'Candela
Flying Chicken
Galapagos Café
Rapa Nui
San Chae Dol Sot Restaurant
Semiramis
Thai Valley
Tre Kronor

ANDERSONVILLE
Ann Sather
Icosium Kafé
Mista
Noodle Zone
Ranalli's of Andersonville
Sabai Dee
Sunshine Café
Taste of Lebanon

BACK OF THE YARDS
Amelia's

BRIDGEPORT
Ed's Potsticker House
Gio's Café & Deli
Healthy Food Lithuanian
    Restaurant
Stages

BUCKTOWN
Babylon Eatery
Coast Sushi Bar
Estrella Negra
Honey 1 BBQ
Thai Eatery
Thai Lagoon

CHINATOWN
Café Hoang
Double Li
Dragon Court
Golden Bull
Hing Kee
Joy Yee Noodle
Joy Yee Plus
Ken-Kee
Mandarin Kitchen
The Noodle
Seven Treasures
Shui Wah
Spring World

EAST UKRAINIAN VILLAGE
El Veneno Mariscos
Jose's Restaurant

EDGEWATER
Antica Pizzeria
Ben's Noodles and Rice
Blue Elephant

Côtes du Rhône
En•Thai•Ce
Everyday Thai
Lalibela
The Little India
M. Henry
Mei Shung
Real Azteca
Shinobu
Summer Noodle & Rice
Tanoshii
Thai Grill
Turkish Cuisine & Bakery

HUMBOLDT PARK

Borinquen
Cemitas Puebla
CJ's Eatery
Feed
Flying Saucer
Treat

HYDE PARK

Café Corea
Caffe Florian
Cedar's Mediterranean Kitchen
Edwardo's
Kikuya
Medici on 57th
Nile Restaurant
Noodles Etc.
Snail Thai Cuisine
Thai 55
Uncle Joe's

IRVING PARK

Dharma Garden
Hot Doug's
Hot Woks, Cool Sushi
Shokran Moroccan Grill

LAKEVIEW

Adesso
Andalous Moroccan
Ann Sather (3 locations)
Asian Avenue
Asian Mix Café
Azha
The Bagel
Bamboo Garden
Barberry Pan Asian Kitchen
Buena Vista Restaurant
Café Blossom
Café Furaibo
Café Orchid
Casbah Café
Chilam Balam
Cozy Noodles & Rice
Crisp
Duck Walk
El Llano Restaurant
Gino's East
Hatsu Hana
HB Home Bistro
Hiro's Café
Istanbul Restaurant
Jai-Yen Fusion Restaurant
Jim Noodle & Rice
Jitlada Thai House
Joy's Noodles & Rice
Kanok
Kitchenette
Late Night Thai
Los Caminos de Michoacan
Machu Picchu
Mark's Chop Suey
Matsu Yama
Miss Asia
Mista
New Jeanny's Restaurant
New Tokyo
90 Miles Cuban Café
Nookies Tree

Oh Fusion
Orange
Papacito's Mexican Grille
Penny's Noodle Shop
Pizza Rustica
Radhuni
Sapore di Napoli
Satay
Standard India
Star of India
Sushi 28 Café
Sweet Tamarind
Ta Tong
TAC Quick Thai Kitchen
Tango Sur
Terragusto
Thai Classic
Thai Thank You
Wings O' Flavor
Yummy Yummy

LINCOLN PARK

Aloha Eats
El Presidente
Ethan's Café
Fattoush
Hema's Kitchen II
Indian Grill
Karyn's Fresh Corner Café
Kyoto Sushi
Lincoln Park's Noodle House
Little Brother's
Mamacita's
Nan's Sushi & Chinese
Noodles in the Pot
Nookies Too
Oodles of Noodles
P.S. Bangkok 2
Robinson's No. 1 Ribs
    Lincoln Park
Simply It

Smoke Shack
Sultan's Market
Sushi Mon
Sushi II Para
Tomato Head
Toro Sushi

LINCOLN SQUARE

Balkan Restaurant
I Monelli Trattoria Pizzeria
Los Nopales
Opart Thai House
Rosded
Royal Thai
Spoon Thai
Thai Oscar
Yes Thai

LOGAN SQUARE

Anong Thai
Atlas Café
Bonsoirée
Café Bella
Charley Thai Place
Ecuador Restaurant
El Rinconcito Cubano
Gloria's Café
Knew
La Cocina de Galarza
    Restaurant
90 Miles Cuban Café
Real Tenochtitlan
The Spice Fusion Thai &
    Japanese Cuisine
Tamalli
Urban Belly

THE LOOP

Ruby of Siam
Siam Rice Thai Cuisine

MAYFAIR
Ay Ay Picante

MCKINLEY PARK
La Palapa
35th Street Café

NEAR NORTH
Panang
Quang

NOBLE SQUARE
Kin Sushi and Thai
Manee Thai #2
Marrakech Cuisine

NORTH CENTER
Always Thai
Sticky Rice
T-Spot Sushi & Tea Bar

NORTH PARK
So Gong Dong Tofu Restaurant

NORTHWEST SIDE
Amira's Trio
Café Marbella
Chai Thai Bistro
Couscous House
The Elephant
Halina's Polish Delights
Jasmine Rice
Noodles Party
Pizza by Alex
Smak Tak
Villa Rosa

OLD IRVING PARK
Siam Taste Noodle
Smoque BBQ
Thai Aree

OLD TOWN
Café Sushi
Garlic & Chili
Lan's
Nookies
Old Jerusalem
Shiso
Thai Aroma

PILSEN
Ciao Amore
Fogata Village
Honky Tonk BBQ
La Cebollita Grill
May Street Café
Nuevo Léon Restaurant
Take Me Out Let's Eat Chinese!

RAVENSWOOD
Aroy Thai
Caro Mio Italian Ristorante
Dorado
Grand Katachi
Isla Pilipina
La Amistad
La Sierra
Le Gee
Mixteco Grill
Mythos
Over Easy Café
Pizza Art Café
Restaurant Sarajevo
Roong Petch
Sabor A Cuba
Siam Country
Thai on Clark
Umaiya Café

RIVER NORTH
Kan Zaman
Rosati's
Yolk

RIVER WEST
Butterfly Sushi Bar &
   Thai Cuisine
Orange
Sushi X

ROGERS PARK
Grande Noodles & Sushi Bar
Habibi
Indie Café
La Cazuela Mariscos
Le Conakry
Luzzat Restaurant
Masouleh
Rice Thai
Sabor Michoacán
Sahara Kabob
Tamales Lo Mejor de Guerrero
Taste of Peru
Thai Spice

ROSCOE VILLAGE
Thai Linda Café

SOUTH LOOP
Café Mediterra
Café Society
Chutney Joe's
The India Grill
Trattoria Caterina
Yolk

SOUTH SIDE
Café 103
Café Trinidad
El Veneno Mariscos

5 Loaves Eatery
Kapeekoo
Sikia
Uncle Joe's (2 locations)
Yassa

UKRAINIAN VILLAGE
Bite Café
Greek Corner

UNIVERSITY VILLAGE/
LITTLE ITALY
Couscous
De Pasada
Golden Thai
Joy Yee Noodle
Lemongrass
Taj Mahal
Thai Bowl
Yummy Thai

UPTOWN
B and Q Afro Root Cuisine
Café Hoang
Café Too
Chinese Kitchen
Dib
Hamamatsu
King of Thai
Le's Pho
New Saigon
Pho 888
Pho 777
Pho Viet
Pho Xe Lua
Pho Xua
Rolis Restaurant
Siam Café
Siam Noodle & Rice
Tank Noodle
Thai Aroma
Thai Avenue

Thai Binh
Thai Pastry
Thai Uptown

WEST LOOP
The Grocery Bistro
Teena Mia
Tomato Head

WEST ROGERS PARK
Ben Tre Café & Restaurant
Bhabi's Kitchen
Chopal Kabab & Steak
Hashalom Restaurant
Hema's Kitchen
Mysore Woodlands
Pizzeria Calzone
Sher-A-Punjab
Taboun Grill
Udupi Palace
Uncle's Kabab
Uru-Swati
Zapp

WEST TOWN
Butterfly Sushi Bar &
    Thai Cuisine
Café Central
Gaudi Coffee and Grill
Habana Libre
Shokolad
Tulum Grill

WICKER PARK
Birchwood Kitchen
Café Con Leche
Irazu
La Fonda del Gusto
Luc Thang
Lucia's Ristorante
Mado
Pot Pan
Schwa
Sultan's Market
Thai Village

Suburbs

EVANSTON
Cozy Noodles & Rice
Joy Yee Noodle
Olive Mountain
Phoenix Inn
Pine Yard
Pinto Thai Kitchen
Pomegranate
Zoba the Noodle Shop

FOREST PARK
Yum Thai

HARWOOD HEIGHTS
Thai Pastry 2

LINCOLNWOOD
Hoanh Long
Wholly Frijoles

NAPERVILLE
Joy Yee Noodle

NORTHFIELD
Penny's Noodle Shop

OAK PARK
Buzz Café
Grape Leaves

SKOKIE
Ruby of Siam
Taboun Grill

PALOS HEIGHTS
Thai Smile

WILMETTE
Tomato Head

SCHAUMBURG
L'Olivo

BYOB Restaurants by Cuisine

AFRICAN
B and Q Afro Root Cuisine
Le Conakry
Sikia
Yassa

Nookies
Nookies Too
Nookies Tree
Stages
Tulum Grill

ALGERIAN
Icosium Kafé

ARGENTINIAN
Tango Sur

AMERICAN
Buzz Café
Caffe Florian
CJ's Eatery
Feed
5 Loaves Eatery
Healthy Food Lithuanian
    Restaurant
La Amistad
Medici on 57th

BBQ
Honey 1 BBQ
Honky Tonk BBQ
Robinson's No. 1 Ribs
    Lincoln Park
Smoke Shack
Smoque BBQ

BOSNIAN
Restaurant Sarajevo

BRUNCH

Adesso
Amelia's
Ann Sather (4 locations)
The Bagel
Birchwood Kitchen
Bite Café
Buzz Café
Café Bella
Café Con Leche
Café 103
Café Too
Caffe Florian
CJ's Eatery
Estrella Negra
Feed
5 Loaves Eatery
Flying Saucer
Fogata Village
Gaudi Coffee and Grill
Icosium Kafé
Istanbul Restaurant
Karyn's Fresh Corner Café
La Sierra
Los Nopales
M. Henry
Medici on 57th
Mixteco Grill
Nookies
Nookies Too
Nookies Tree
Orange (2 locations)
Over Easy Café
Rolis Restaurant
Shokolad
Sikia
Taboun Grill (2 locations)
Tre Kronor
Treat
Tulum Grill
Yolk (2 locations)

CARIBBEAN

Café Trinidad
Kapeekoo
Uncle Joe's (3 locations)

CHILEAN

Rapa Nui

CHINESE

Bamboo Garden
Chinese Kitchen
Double Li
Dragon Court
Ed's Potsticker House
Golden Bull
Ken-Kee
Lan's
Mandarin Kitchen
Mark's Chop Suey
Mei Shung
Nan's Sushi & Chinese
New Jeanny's Restaurant
Pho Xua
Phoenix Inn
Pine Yard
Seven Treasures
Shui Wah
Spring World

COLOMBIAN

Brasa Roja
El Llano Restaurant
Flying Chicken
Gloria's Café

CONTEMPORARY AMERICAN

Café 103
Café Too

The Grocery Bistro
HB Home Bistro
M. Henry
Orange (2 locations)

COSTA RICAN
Irazu

CUBAN
Amira's Trio
El Rinconcito Cubano
Habana Libre
90 Miles Cuban Café
   (2 locations)
Sabor A Cuba

EASTERN EUROPEAN
Balkan Restaurant

ECLECTIC
Atlas Café
Birchwood Kitchen
Bite Café
Bonsoirée
Café Bella
Café Mediterra
Café Society
Flying Saucer
Hot Doug's
Knew
Mado
Over Easy Café
Schwa
Shokolad
35th Street Café
Treat
Wings O' Flavor
Yolk (2 locations)

ECUADORIAN
Ecuador Restaurant
Galapagos Café

ETHIOPIAN
Lalibela

FRENCH
Côtes du Rhône

GREEK
Greek Corner
Mythos

HAWAIIAN
Aloha Eats

INDIAN
Bhabi's Kitchen
Chopal Kabab & Steak
Chutney Joe's
Hema's Kitchen
Hema's Kitchen II
The India Grill
Indian Grill
The Little India
Luzzat Restaurant
Mysore Woodlands
Radhuni
Sher-A-Punjab
Standard India
Star of India
Taj Mahal
Udupi Palace
Uru-Swati

ISRAELI
Hashalom Restaurant

ITALIAN
Adesso
Antica Pizzeria
Caffe Florian
Caro Mio Italian Ristorante
Ciao Amore
Edwardo's
Gino's East
Gio's Café & Deli
I Monelli Trattoria Pizzeria
L'Olivo
Lucia's Ristorante
Mista (2 locations)
Pizza Art Café
Pizza by Alex
Pizza Rustica
Pizzeria Calzone
Ranalli's of Andersonville
Rosati's
Sapore di Napoli
Teena Mia
Terragusto
Tomato Head (3 locations)
Trattoria Caterina
Villa Rosa

JAPANESE
Asian Avenue
Butterfly Sushi Bar & Thai
   Cuisine (2 locations)
Café Blossom
Café Furaibo
Café Sushi
Coast Sushi Bar
Dib
Ethan's Café
Galapagos Café
Grand Katachi
Grande Noodles & Sushi Bar
Hamamatsu
Hatsu Hana
Hiro's Café

Indie Café
Jai-Yen Fusion Restaurant
Jasmine Rice
Joy Yee Plus
Kikuya
Kin Sushi and Thai
Kitchenette
Kyoto Sushi
Lincoln Park's Noodle House
Matsu Yama
Nan's Sushi & Chinese
New Tokyo
Oh Fusion
Roong Petch
Shinobu
Shiso
The Spice Fusion Thai &
   Japanese Cuisine
Sunshine Café
Sushi Mon
Sushi 28 Café
Sushi II Para
Sushi X
Ta Tong
Tanoshii
Thai Oscar
Thai Spice
Toro Sushi
T-Spot Sushi & Tea Bar

JEWISH
The Bagel

KOREAN
Café Corea
Crisp
Ethan's Café
Hiro's Café
Little Brother's
San Chae Dol Sot Restaurant
So Gong Dong Tofu Restaurant

LAO
Sabai Dee

LITHUANIAN
Healthy Food Lithuanian
   Restaurant

MEDITERRANEAN
Couscous House

MEXICAN
Amelia's
Buena Vista Restaurant
Café Con Leche
Cemitas Puebla
Chilam Balam
De Pasada
El Presidente
El Veneno Mariscos
   (2 locations)
Estrella Negra
Fogata Village
Jose's Restaurant
La Amistad
La Cazuela Mariscos
La Cebollita Grill
La Fonda del Gusto
La Palapa
Los Caminos de Michoacan
Los Nopales
Mamacita's
Nuevo Léon Restaurant
Papacito's Mexican Grille
Real Azteca
Rolis Restaurant
Sabor Michoacán
Tamales Lo Mejor de Guerrero
Tamalli
Tulum Grill
Wholly Frijoles

MIDDLE EASTERN
Babylon Eatery
Casbah Café
Cedar's Mediterranean Kitchen
Couscous
Fattoush
Grape Leaves
Habibi
Kan Zaman
Masouleh
Nile Restaurant
Old Jerusalem
Olive Mountain
Pomegranate
Sahara Kabob
Semiramis
Sultan's Market (2 locations)
Taboun Grill (2 locations)
Taste of Lebanon
Uncle's Kabab

MOROCCAN
Andalous Moroccan
Couscous
Hashalom Restaurant
Marrakech Cuisine
Shokran Moroccan Grill

NUEVO LATINO
Dorado
La Sierra
May Street Café
Mixteco Grill
Real Tenochtitlan

PAKISTANI
Bhabi's Kitchen
Chopal Kabab & Steak
Taj Mahal

PAN-ASIAN
Asian Mix Café
Blue Elephant
Hing Kee
Hot Woks, Cool Sushi
Joy Yee Noodle (4 locations)
Kanok
Le Gee
Luc Thang
Manee Thai #2
Miss Asia
Noodle Zone
Noodles Etc.
Noodles Party
Oodles of Noodles
Pinto Thai Kitchen
Satay
Summer Noodle & Rice
Take Me Out Let's Eat Chinese!
Thai Lagoon
Umaiya Café
Urban Belly
Yummy Yummy
Zoba the Noodle Shop

PERUVIAN
Ay Ay Picante
D'Candela
Machu Picchu
Taste of Peru

PHILIPPINE
Isla Pilipina

POLISH
Halina's Polish Delights
Smak Tak

PUERTO RICAN
Amira's Trio
Borinquen

Café Central
La Cocina de Galarza
    Restaurant

SCANDINAVIAN
Ann Sather (4 locations)
Tre Kronor

SPANISH
Café Marbella
Gaudi Coffee and Grill

TAIWANESE
Mei Shung

THAI
Always Thai
Anong Thai
Aroy Thai
Asian Avenue
Azha
Barberry Pan Asian Kitchen
Ben's Noodles and Rice
Butterfly Sushi Bar & Thai
    Cuisine (2 locations)
Café Hoang (2 locations)
Chai Thai Bistro
Charley Thai Place
Cozy Noodles & Rice
    (2 locations)
Dharma Garden
Dib
Duck Walk
The Elephant
En•Thai•Ce
Everyday Thai
Garlic & Chili
Golden Thai
Grande Noodles & Sushi Bar
Indie Café
Jai-Yen Fusion Restaurant

Jasmine Rice
Jim Noodle & Rice
Jitlada Thai House
Joy's Noodles & Rice
Kin Sushi and Thai
King of Thai
Kitchenette
Late Night Thai
Lemongrass
Lincoln Park's Noodle House
Noodles in the Pot
Oh Fusion
Opart Thai House
Panang
Penny's Noodle Shop
   (2 locations)
Pot Pan
P.S. Bangkok 2
Quang
Rice Thai
Roong Petch
Rosded
Royal Thai
Ruby of Siam (2 locations)
Siam Café
Siam Country
Siam Noodle & Rice
Siam Rice Thai Cuisine
Siam Taste Noodle
Snail Thai Cuisine
The Spice Fusion Thai &
   Japanese Cuisine
Spoon Thai
Sticky Rice
Sweet Tamarind
Ta Tong
TAC Quick Thai Kitchen
Thai Aree
Thai Aroma (2 locations)
Thai Avenue
Thai Bowl
Thai Classic
Thai Eatery

Thai 55
Thai Grill
Thai Linda Café
Thai on Clark
Thai Oscar
Thai Pastry
Thai Pastry 2
Thai Smile
Thai Spice
Thai Thank You
Thai Uptown
Thai Valley
Thai Village
Yes Thai
Yum Thai
Yummy Thai
Zapp

TURKISH
Café Orchid
Istanbul Restaurant
Turkish Cuisine & Bakery

VEGETARIAN
Cousin's Incredible Vitality
Dharma Garden
En•Thai•Ce
Karyn's Fresh Corner Café
Mysore Woodlands
Udupi Palace
Uru-Swati

VIETNAMESE
Ben Tre Café & Restaurant
Big Pho
Café Hoang (2 locations)
Hoanh Long
Joy Yee Plus
Le's Pho
New Saigon
The Noodle

Pho 888
Pho 777
Pho Viet
Pho Xe Lua
Pho Xua

Quang
Simply It
Sushi 28 Café
Tank Noodle
Thai Binh

BYOB Restaurants by Feature

OUTDOOR SEATING

Adesso
Amira's Trio
Andalous Moroccan
Ann Sather (Lakeview/
 Southport)
Ay Ay Picante
Babylon Eatery
Birchwood Kitchen
Blue Elephant
Bonsoirée
Buena Vista Restaurant
Butterfly Sushi Bar & Thai
 Cuisine (2 locations)
Buzz Café
Café Blossom
Café Con Leche
Café Society
Café Sushi
Café Too
Chutney Joe's
Cozy Noodles & Rice
 (Lakeview)
El Presidente
El Veneno Mariscos (East
 Ukrainian Village)

Ethan's Café
Feed
Gaudi Coffee and Grill
Gino's East
Greek Corner
The Grocery Bistro
Hot Doug's
Hot Woks, Cool Sushi
I Monelli Trattoria Pizzeria
Irazu
Jim Noodle & Rice
Joy Yee Noodle (Evanston)
Joy's Noodles & Rice
Kan Zaman
Karyn's Fresh Corner Café
Knew
La Cazuela Mariscos
La Cocina de Galarza
 Restaurant
La Palapa
Lucia's Ristorante
M. Henry
Medici on 57th
Mista (2 locations)
Mythos

New Tokyo
90 Miles Cuban Café (2
    locations)
Noodles in the Pot
Nookies
Nookies Tree
Oh Fusion
Old Jerusalem
Orange (2 locations)
Papacito's Mexican Grille
Penny's Noodle Shop
    (Lakeview)
Pizza Art Café
Pizza Rustica
Ranalli's of Andersonville
Rice Thai
Robinson's No. 1 Ribs
    Lincoln Park
Rosati's
Sabor A Cuba
Shokolad
Siam Country
Sticky Rice
Sultan's Market (Wicker Park)
Sweet Tamarind
Ta Tong
TAC Quick Thai Kitchen
Tango Sur
Thai Bowl
Thai Linda Café
Thai Village
35th Street Café
Trattoria Caterina
Tre Kronor
Treat
T-Spot Sushi & Tea Bar
Wholly Frijoles
Yes Thai

PRIVATE PARTY ROOM
Ann Sather (Lakeview/
    Belmont)
Caro Mio Italian Restaurant
Dharma Garden
Estrella Negra
Hing Kee
Joy Yee Noodle (Chinatown)
Joy Yee Plus
Kyoto Sushi
La Fonda del Gusto
Le Conakry
Lincoln Park's Noodle House
Los Nopales
Real Tenochtitlan
Rolis Restaurant
Satay
Thai Grill
35th Street Café

Chicago Neighborhoods

1. West Rogers Park
2. Rogers Park
3. Edgewater/ Andersonville
4. Mayfair
5. Old Irving Park
6. Irving Park
7. Albany Park
8. Lincoln Square/ Ravenswood
9. Uptown
10. North Center
11. Roscoe Village
12. Lakeview
13. Logan Square
14. Bucktown
15. Humboldt Park
16. Wicker Park
17. Ukrainian Village
18. East Ukrainian Village
19. Noble Square/ West Town
20. Lincoln Park
21. Old Town
22. Gold Coast
23. Near North
24. River West
25. River North
26. Greektown
27. West Loop
28. Loop
29. Streeterville
30. South Loop/ Printer's Row
31. University Village/ Little Italy
32. Pilsen
33. Chinatown
34. Bridgeport
35. Little Village
36. Hyde Park

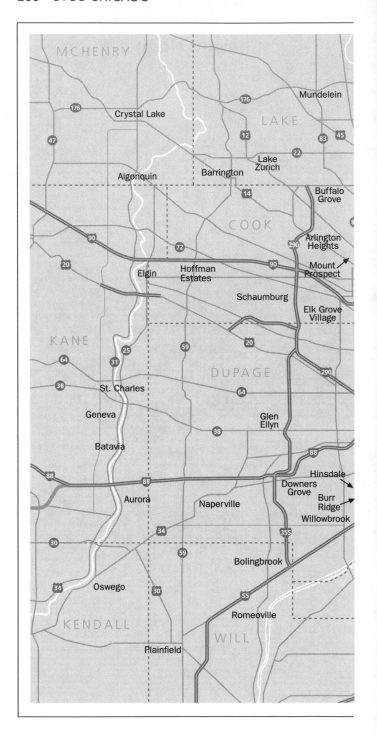

Chicago & Vicinity

Lake Forest

Lincolnshire

Deerfield

Highland Park

Glencoe

Northbrook

Wheeling

Glenview

Wilmette

Evanston

Des Plaines

Niles

Skokie

LAKE MICHIGAN

Lincolnwood

Rosemont

River Grove

Elmwood Park

Oak Park

CHICAGO

Forest Park

Berwyn

Evergreen Park

Oak Lawn

Blue Island

Orland Park

Tinley Park

ILLINOIS

BYOB Chicago℠:
Now it's everywhere you go.

BYOB Chicago: Your Guide to Bring-Your-Own-Bottle Restaurants and Wine & Spirits Stores in Chicago, 3rd Edition, is available in eBook format at Amazon.com's Kindle Store, BarnesandNoble.com, eBookStore.Sony.com, eBooks.com, LightningSource.com, Powells.com, and your favorite library wholesaler.

BYOB Chicago eBooks can also be read on the iPhone/ iPod Touch when purchased at Amazon.com's Kindle Store (apps are available at Apple.com's App Store), and your iPhone/iPod Touch, Blackberry®, PC, or Mac when purchased at BarnesandNoble.com (download the free eReader at BarnesandNoble.com).

Planning a special event? *BYOB Chicago*'s author Jean Iversen is available for presentations, speaking engagements, and classes for:

- Wine clubs
- Wine tastings
- Beer tastings
- Wine classes
- BYOB clubs
- Special events
- Corporate events
- Wine festivals
- Beer festivals
- Book signings
- Bookstore events
- Publishing/Author events

Please contact info@byobchicago.com for more information.

BYOB-Chicago.com